I0489333

Elmira Ontario Book 2, Hawkesville, and Wallenstein in Colour Photos, Saving Our History One Photo at a Time

Photography
by Barbara Raué
2014

Series Name:
Cruising Ontario

Book 71: Elmira Book 2,
Hawkesville, and Wallenstein

Cover photo: 42 Church Street West, Elmira

Series Name: Cruising Ontario
Saving Our History One Photo at a Time

Other Books by Barbara Raue

Coins of Gold

Arrows, Indians and Love

The Life and Times of Barbara
Volume 1: Inventions That Have Enhanced My Life
Volume 2: Entertainment That I Have Enjoyed
Volume 3: East Coast Trips
Volume 4: Olympics Have Always Intrigued Me
Volume 5: Wonders of the World
Volume 6: Caribbean Cruises We Have Enjoyed
Volume 7: Animals
Volume 8: Storms and Other Major Disasters in My Lifetime
Volume 9: Wars, Terrorist Attacks and Major Disasters

The Cromwell Family Book

Laura Secord Discovered

Visit Barbara's website to view all of her books
http://barbararaue.ericraue.com

Elmira

Elmira is the largest community within the Township of Woolwich in the Regional Municipality of Waterloo and is located 15 kilometres (9 miles) to the north of the city of Waterloo.

The land comprising Woolwich Township originally belonged to the Huron and then the Mohawk Indians. The first settlers arrived in Woolwich Township in the late eighteenth century. In 1798, William Wallace, one of the first settlers in the area, was deeded 86,078 acres of land on the Grand River for a cost of $16,364.

In 1806, Wallace sold the major portion of his tract to Mennonites. Benjamin Eby, the secretary of the Germany Company came to the area with his friend Henry Brubacher. The young men liked Wallace's Woolwich. Eby returned to Pennsylvania where he formed a land company. The following year, he returned with a barrel of silver dollars, and the Musselmans, Martins, Hoffmans, and Gingerichs to settle in the area. Wallace sold the Germany Company 45,185 acres of land at $1.00 an acre.

In 1834, Edward Bristow became one of Elmira's first settlers when he purchased 53 acres of land here for 50 cents per acre. A community by the name of Bristow's Corners was in existence in 1839 when a post office was assigned there. In 1853 the community was renamed Elmira. In the 1850s, German settlers moved into the community, including Oswald, Esche, Steffen and Tresinger. Like most of the township, the primary settlers in the Elmira area were Mennonites who still form a significant proportion of the population today. The town still retains much of its traditional Pennsylvania Dutch character.

Hawkesville

The Township of Wellesley is the rural, north-western township of the Regional Municipality of Waterloo. The township comprises the communities of Bamberg, Crosshill, Hawkesville, Heidelberg, Kingwood, Knight's Corners, Linwood, Macton, St. Clements, Wallenstein and Wellesley.

Hawkesville never got the railroad. On a hill itself, ringed by the flat of the Conestogo River, itself inside a ring of tall hills, it was deemed too difficult a task to bring the trains through town. Hawkesville has maintained the charm of the surrounding sugar maple woods and the quiet river banks.

Wellesley Township was surveyed in 1842, but settlers were in this area long before. In 1837, John Philip Schweitzer from Germany squatted at what is now Hawkesville, and had 40 acres of land cleared over the following nine years. Then, John Hawke received government permission to buy the clearing for $700.00 on the condition that he build a grist mill for flour and a sawmill within two years.

When the Waterloo County boundaries were established in 1852 to include the townships of Waterloo, Wellesley, Wilmot, Woolwich, and North Dumfries, John Hawke was named the first reeve of Wellesley and the first township hall was built in Hawkesville. When the decision was being made for the location of a county seat, Hawkesville originally anticipated being chosen over Berlin and Galt. However, John Hawke had the deciding vote, and he cast it in favour of Berlin. With the railroad and the county seat, Berlin began to grow rapidly and kept on growing; Hawkesville flourished until the end of the century before diminishing.

Before the dawning of the 20th century, the area was home to doctors, blacksmiths, and merchants, as well as a tannery, hotels, and churches. Into the early 1900s, the village carriage and wagon maker, George Diefenbacker entertained his grandson, John Diefenbaker, each summer.

Table of Contents

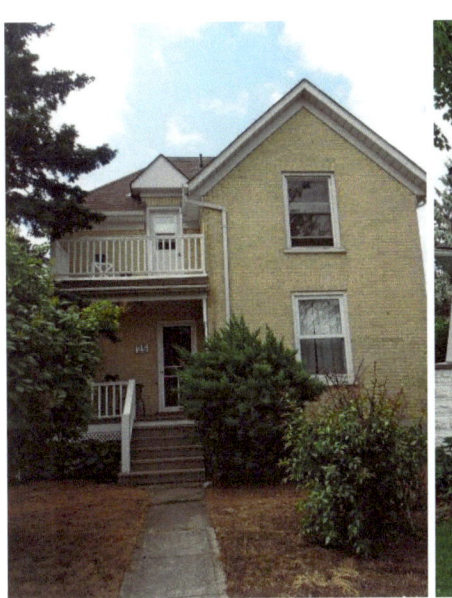

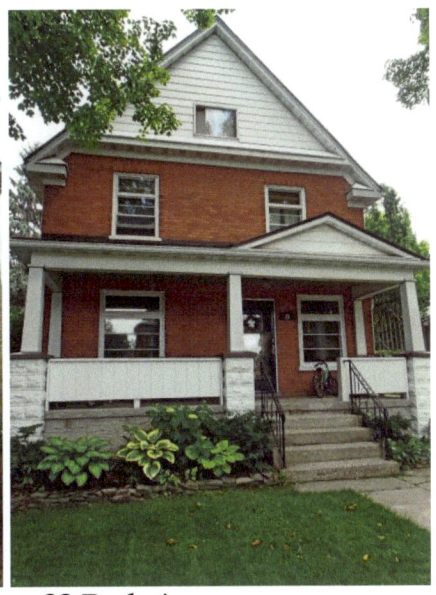

25 Park Avenue

22 Park Avenue
Edwardian, pediment,
Cornice return on gable

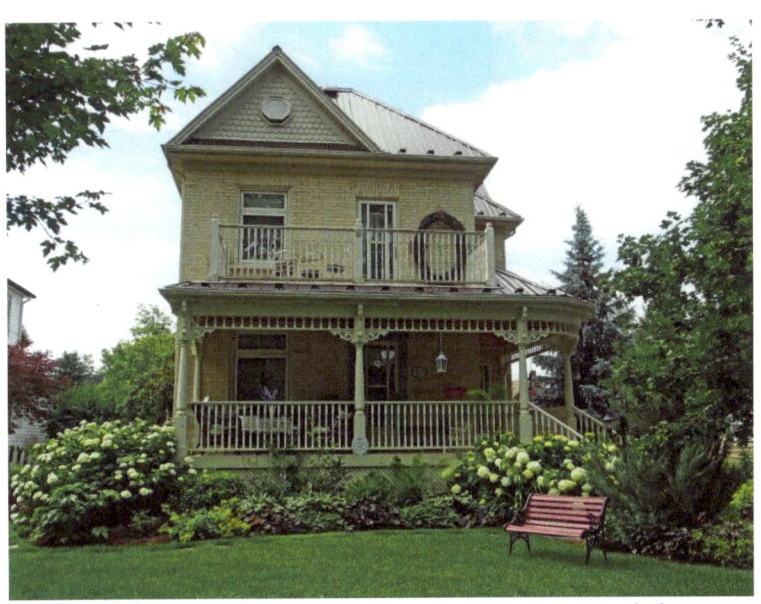

23 Park Avenue – balcony above verandah

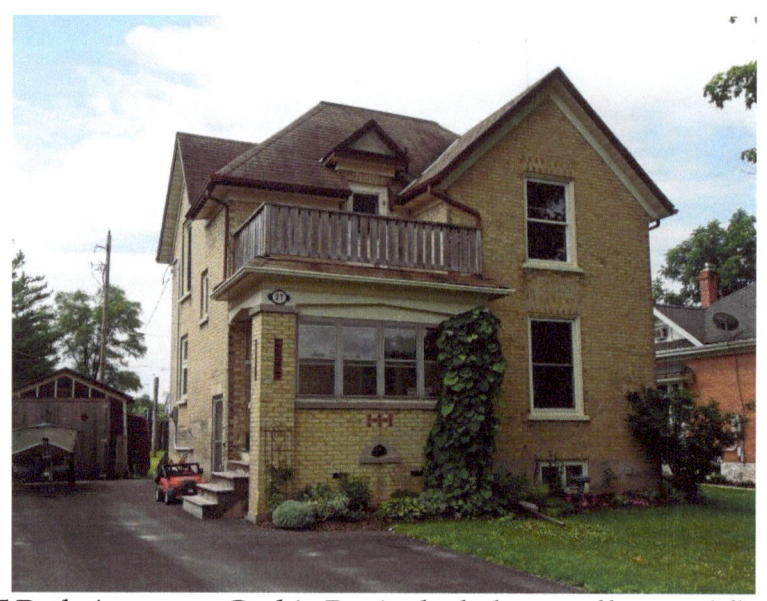

27 Park Avenue – Gothic Revival – balcony off second floor

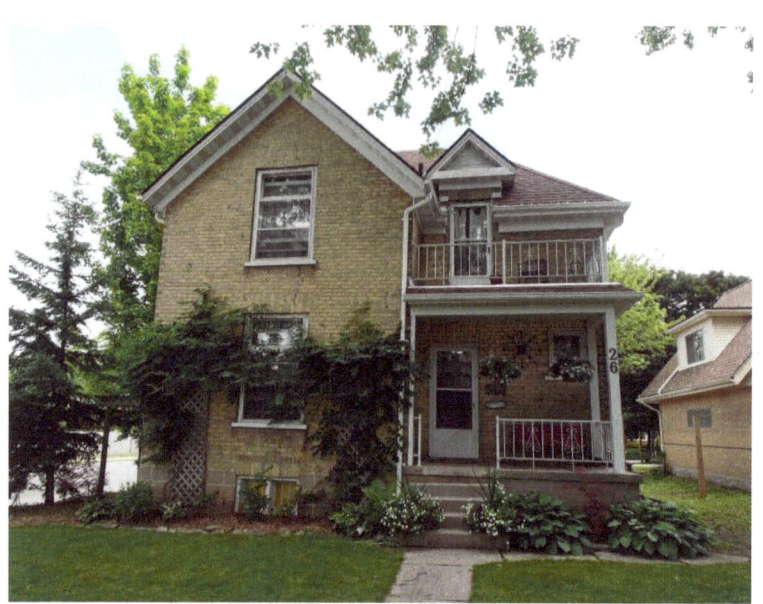

26 Park Avenue – Gothic Revival

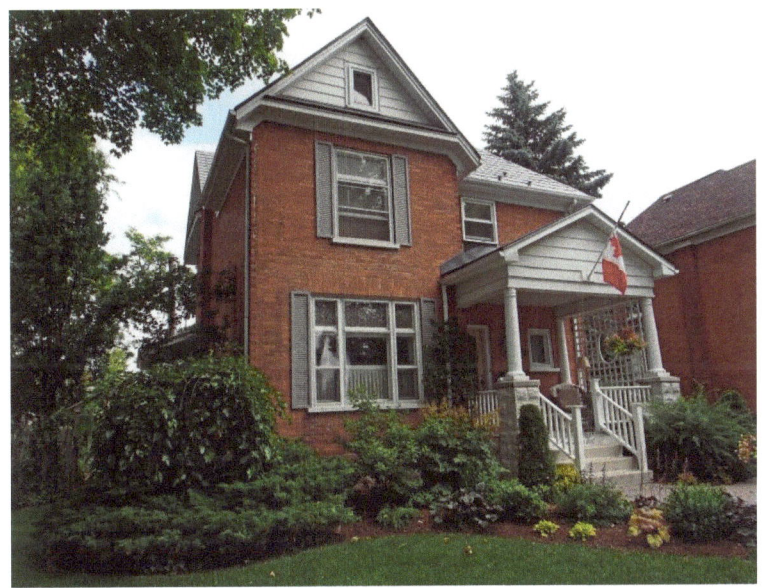

Edwardian

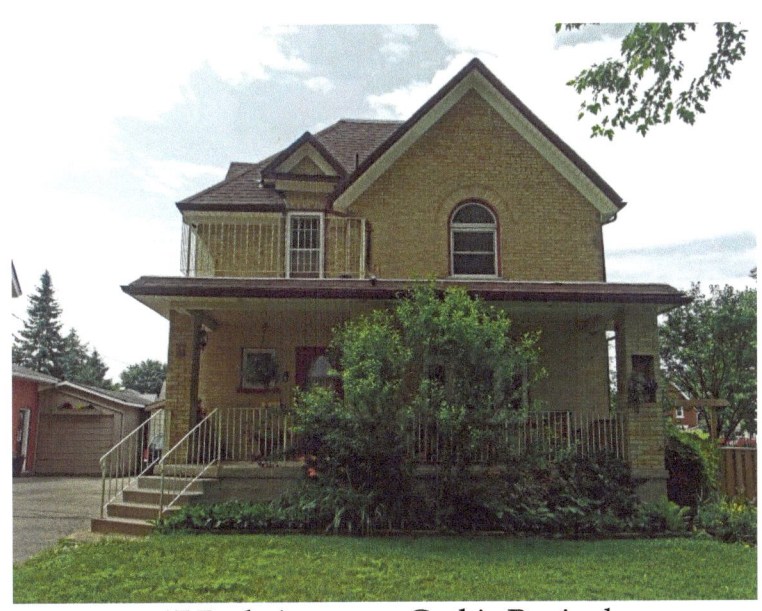

17 Park Avenue – Gothic Revival

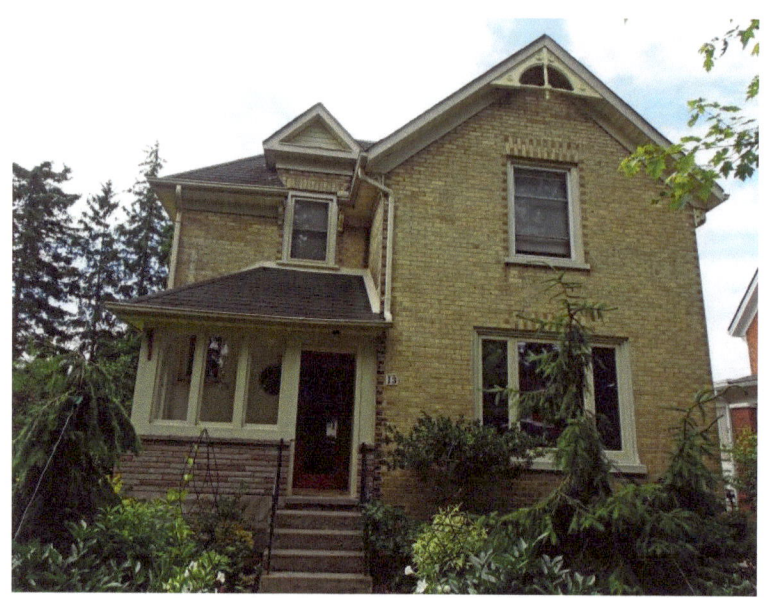

13 Park Avenue – Gothic Revival

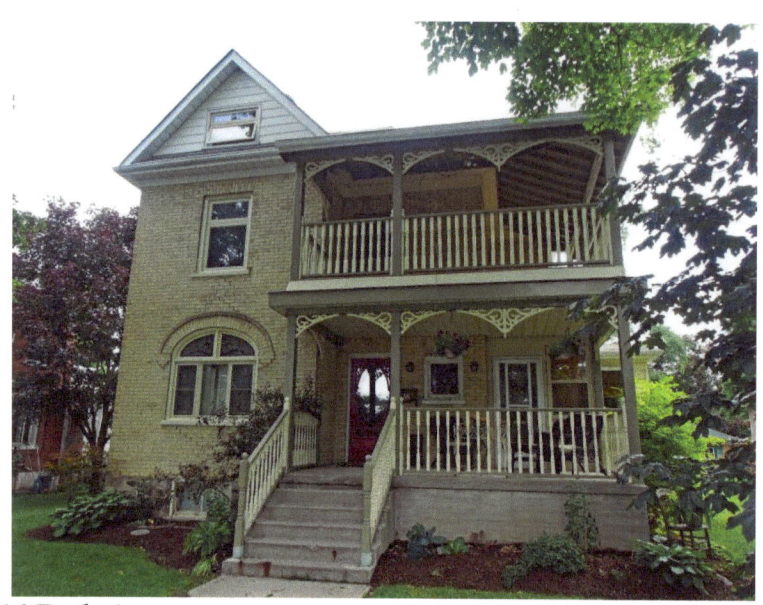

16 Park Avenue – wraparound verandahs on both levels

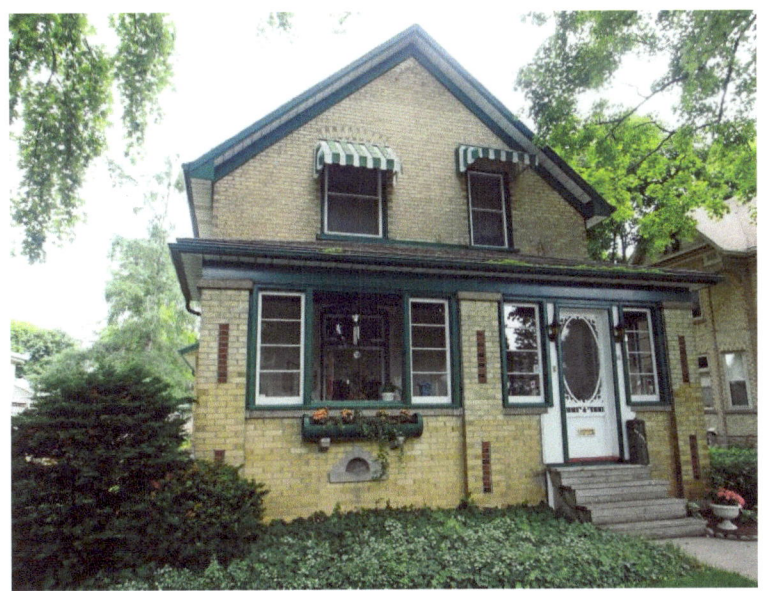

14 Park Avenue – Gothic Revival

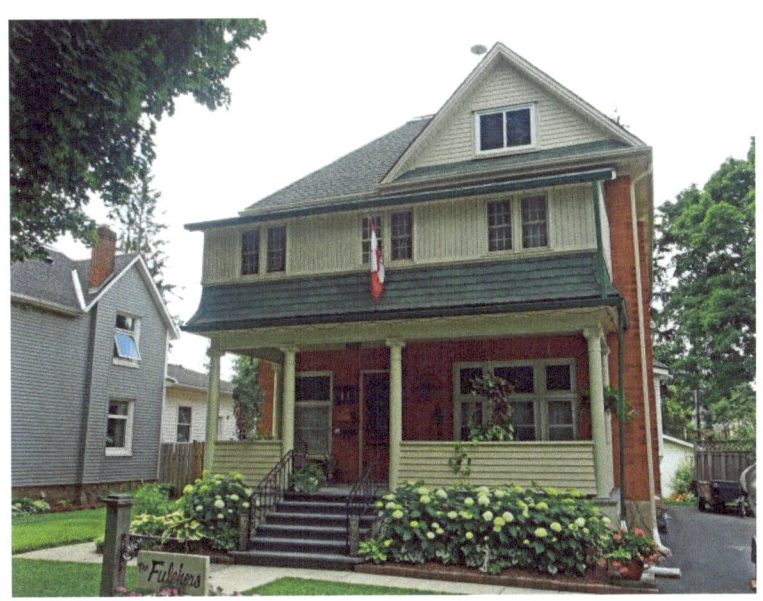

11 Park Avenue - Edwardian

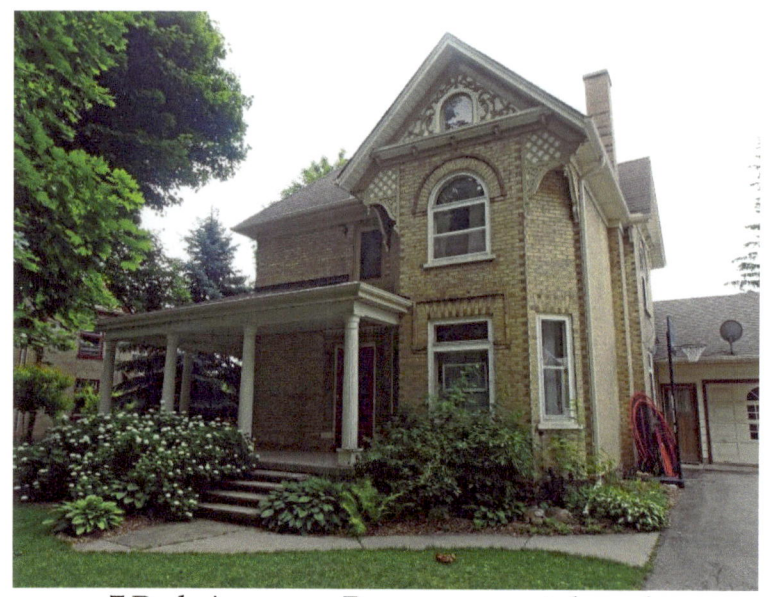

7 Park Avenue – Romanesque style arch
on second floor window, fretwork

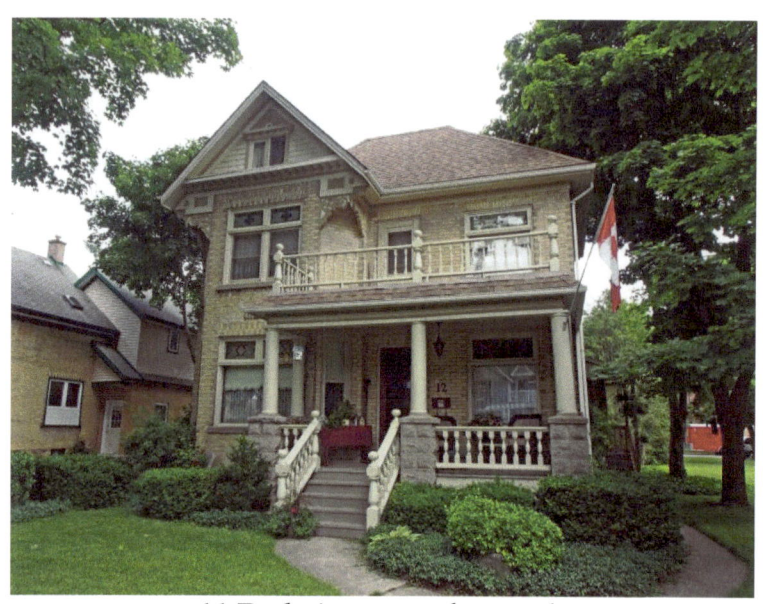

11 Park Avenue - fretwork

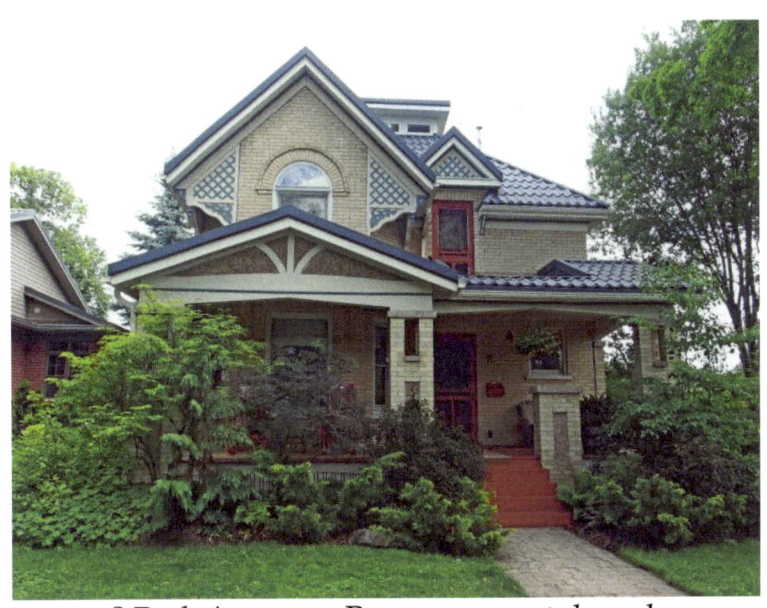

8 Park Avenue – Romanesque style arch
on second floor window

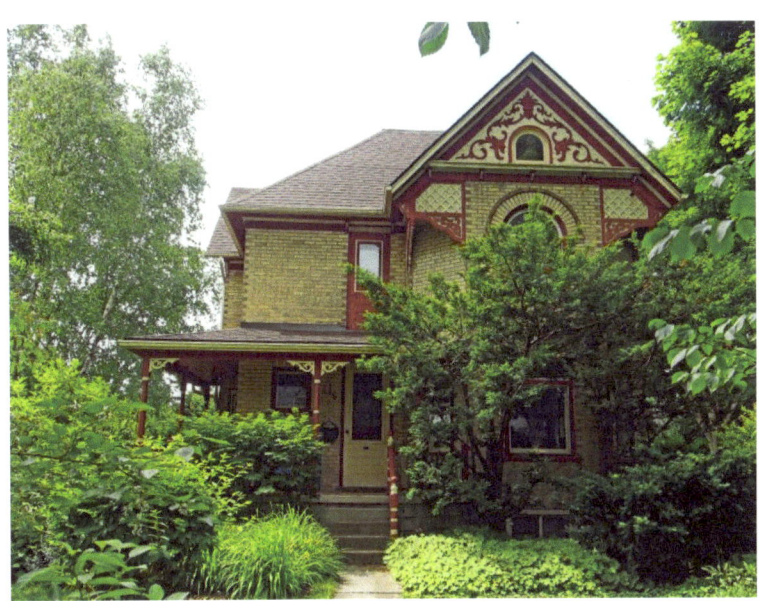

5 Park Avenue – decorative gable, Romanesque style arch
on second floor window

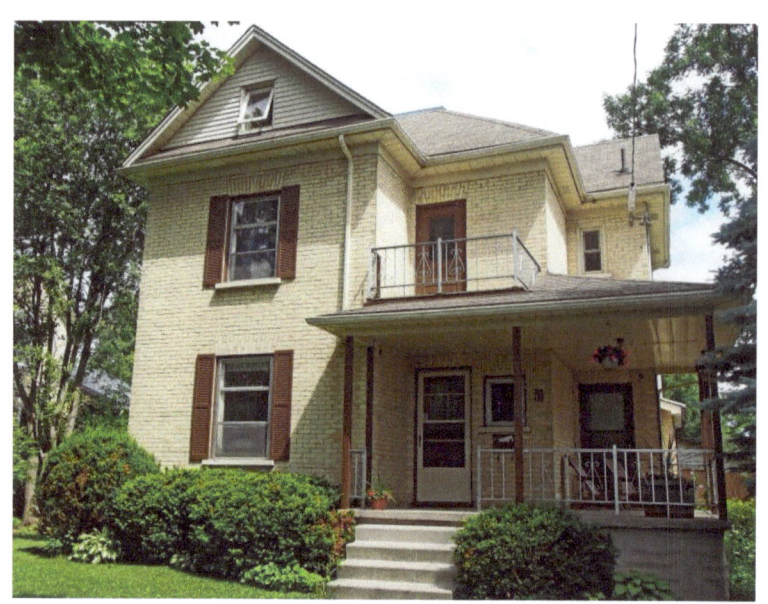

6 Park Avenue

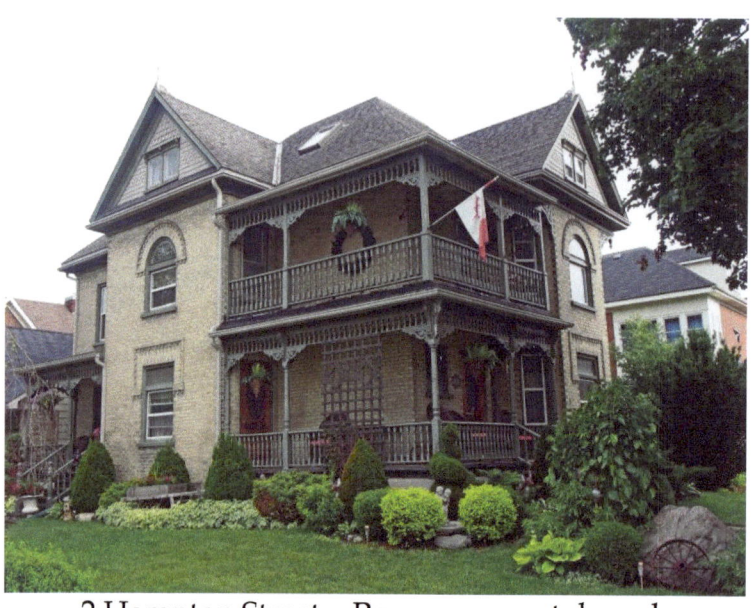

2 Hampton Street – Romanesque style arch
on second floor window

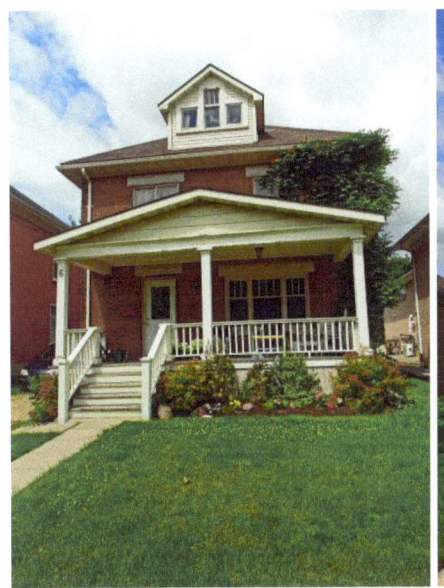

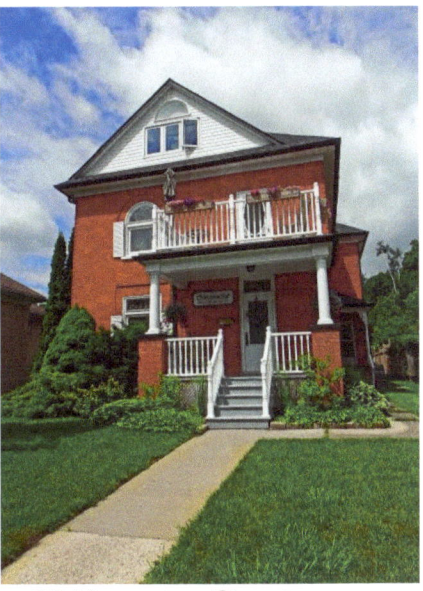

6 Hampton Street
Italianate, dormer in attic
with Palladian window

10 Hampton Street
Edwardian, 2nd floor balcony
Palladian window

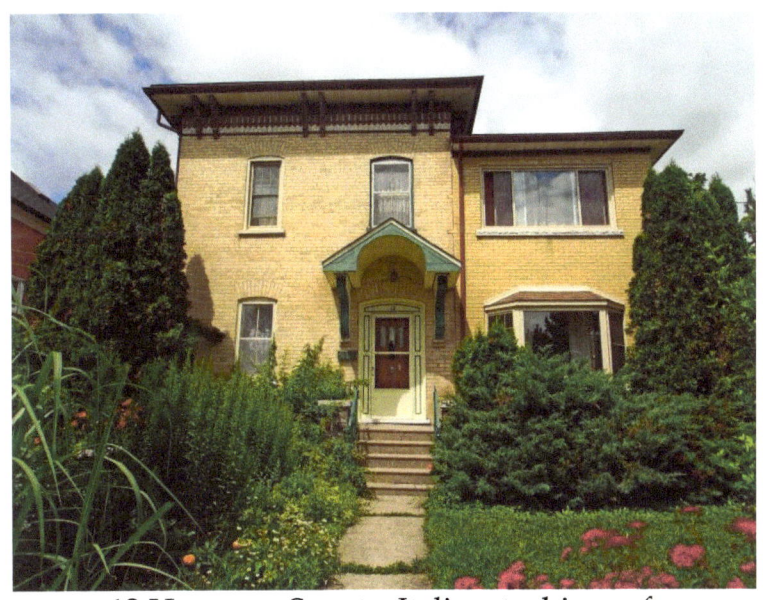

12 Hampton Street – Italianate, hip roof,
paired cornice brackets

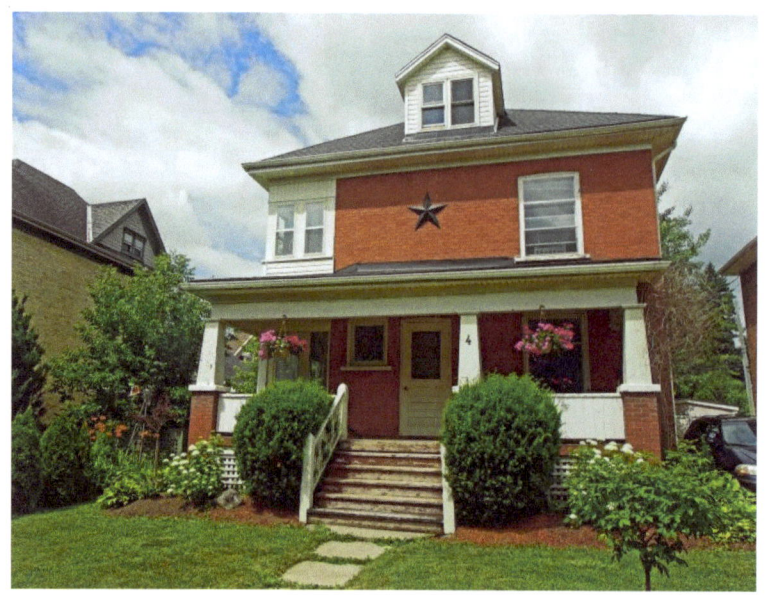

4 Hampton Street – Italianate - dormer

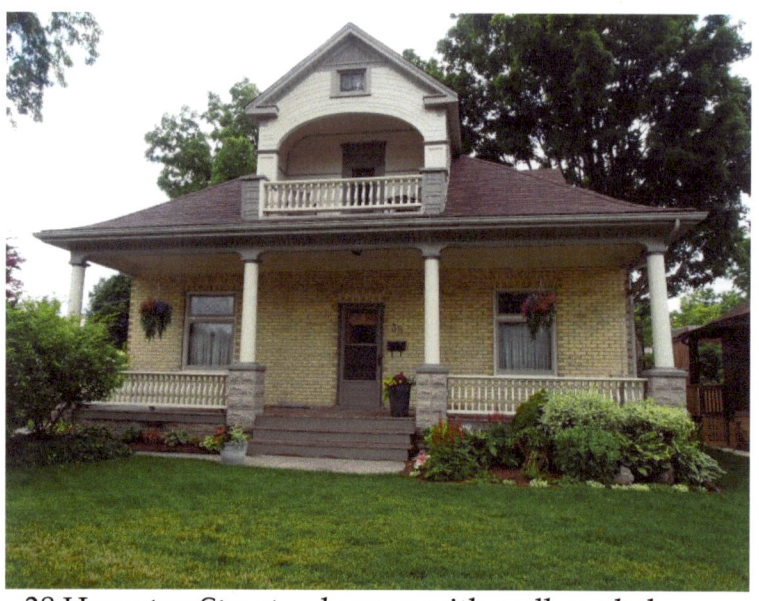

38 Hampton Street – dormer with walkout balcony,
cornice return on gable

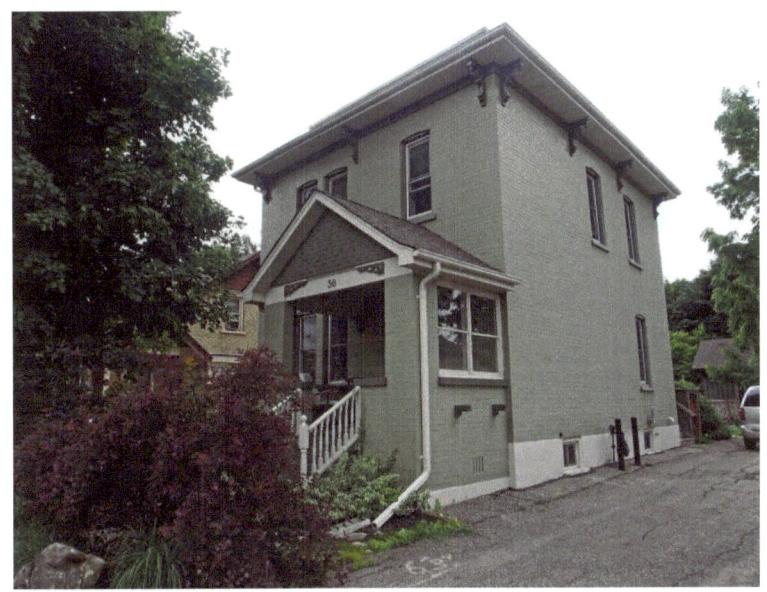

36 Hampton Street – Italianate, cornice brackets

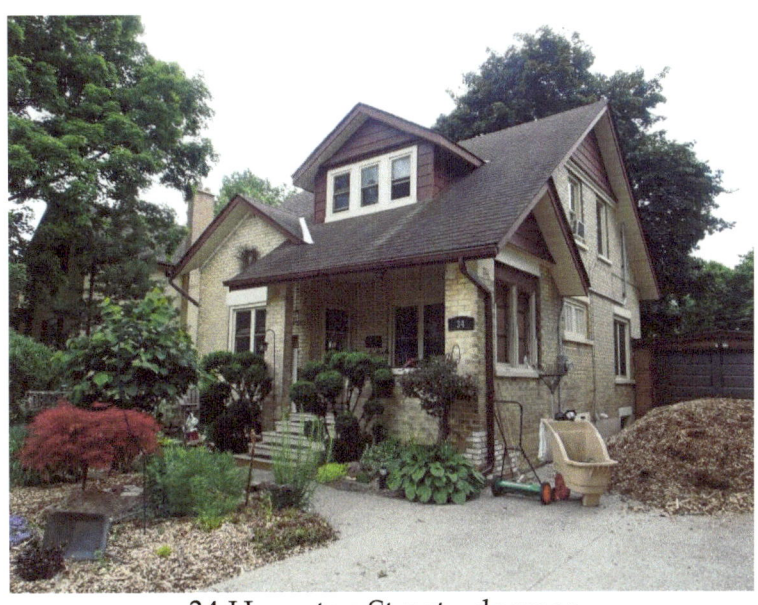

34 Hampton Street - dormer

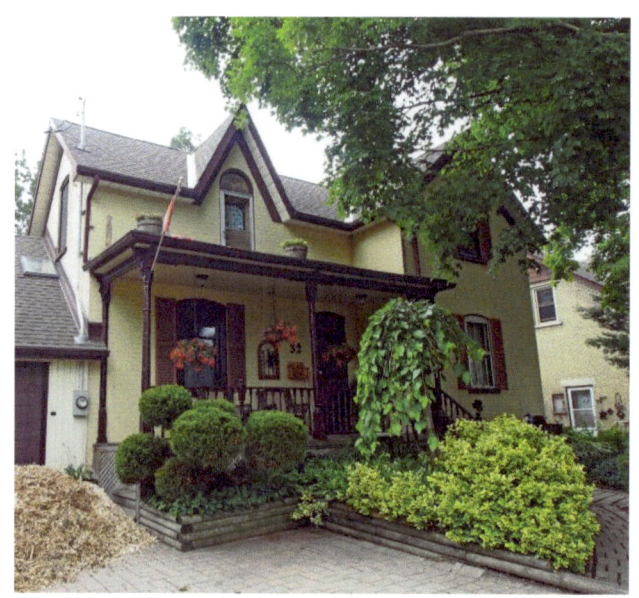

32 Hampton Street – Gothic Revival

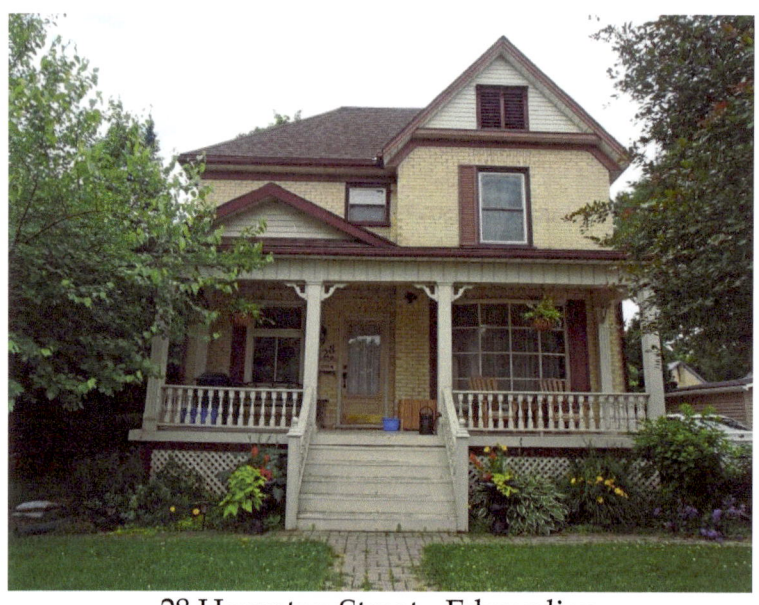

28 Hampton Street - Edwardian

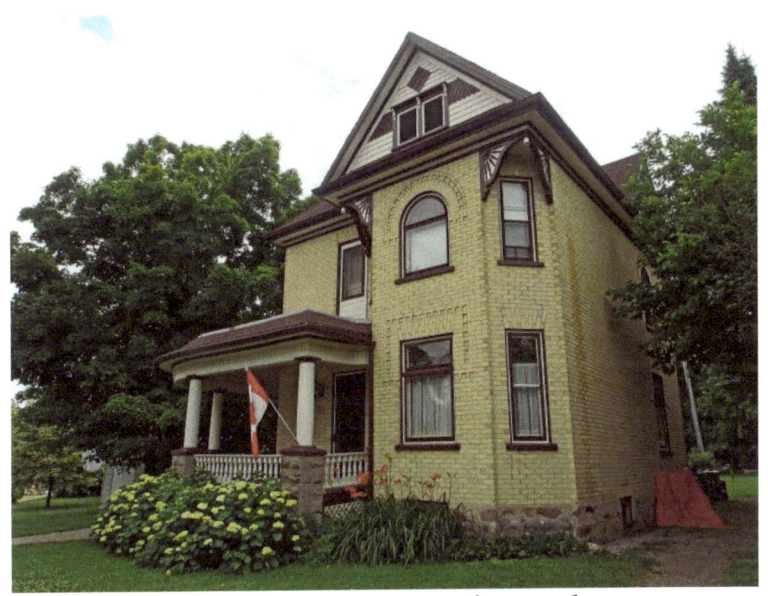

26 Hampton Street - fretwork

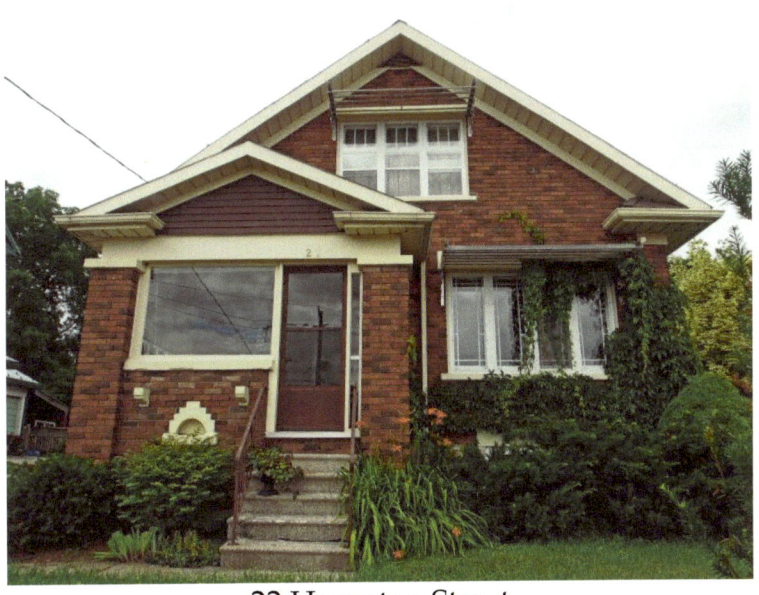

22 Hampton Street

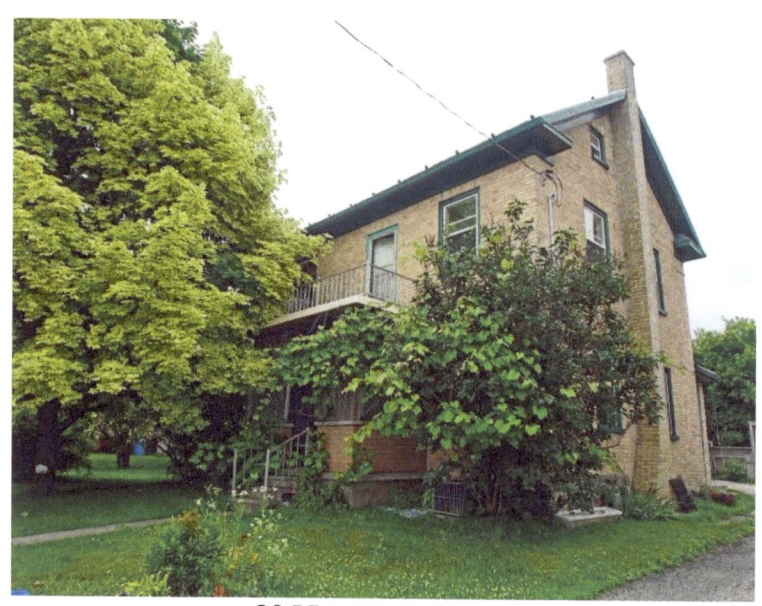

20 Hampton Street

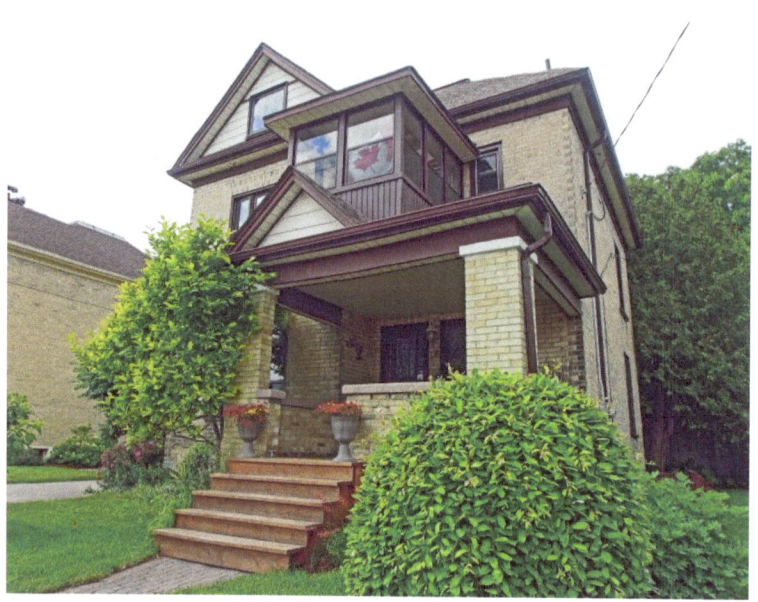

18 Hampton Street

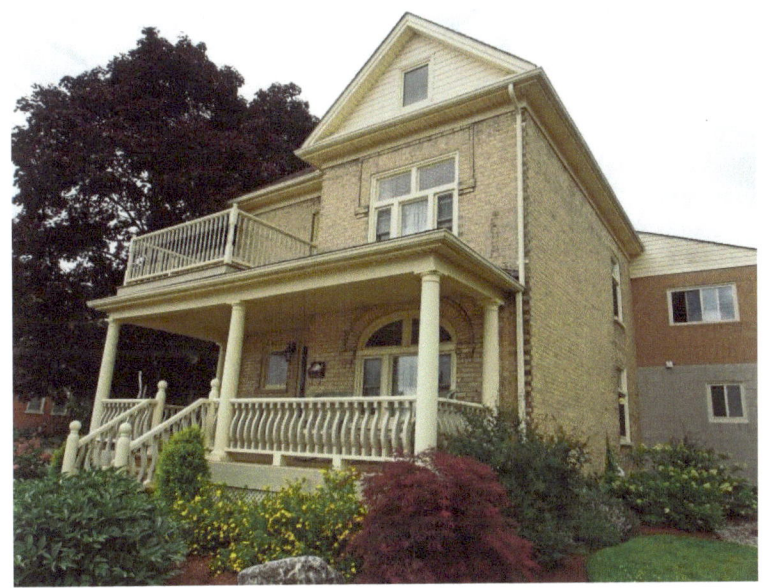

16 Hampton Street

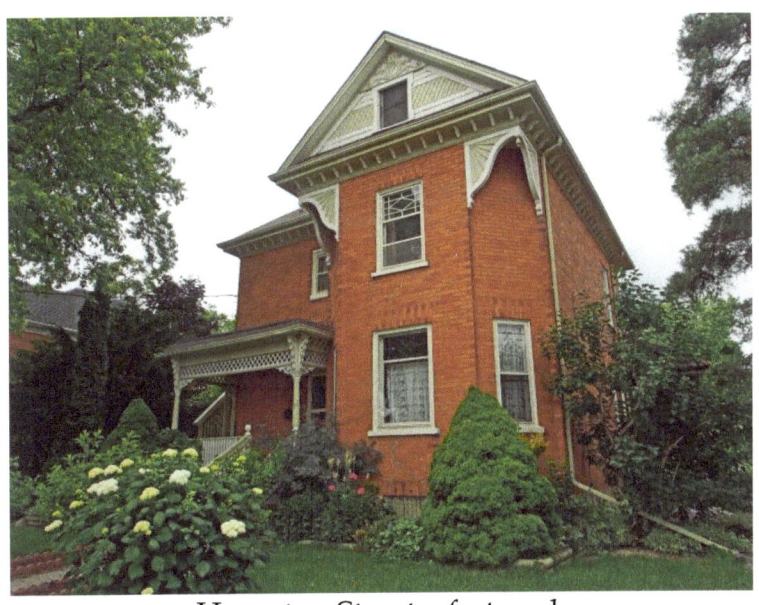

Hampton Street – fretwork

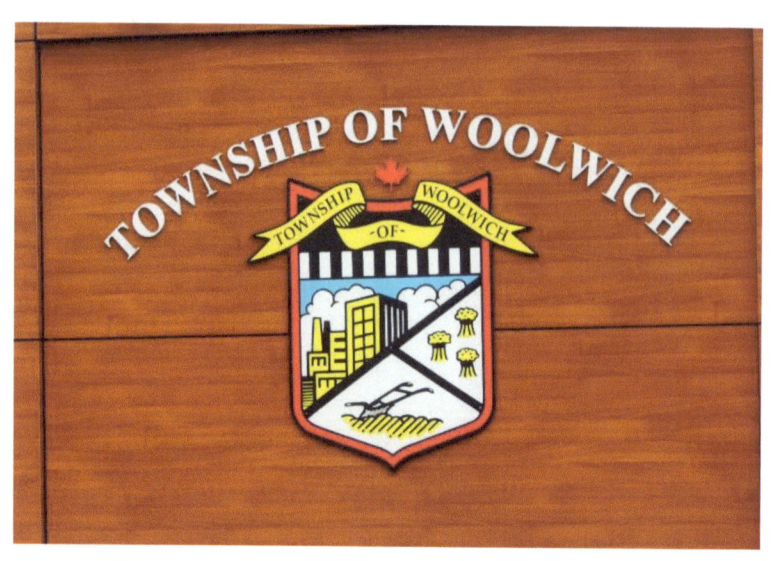

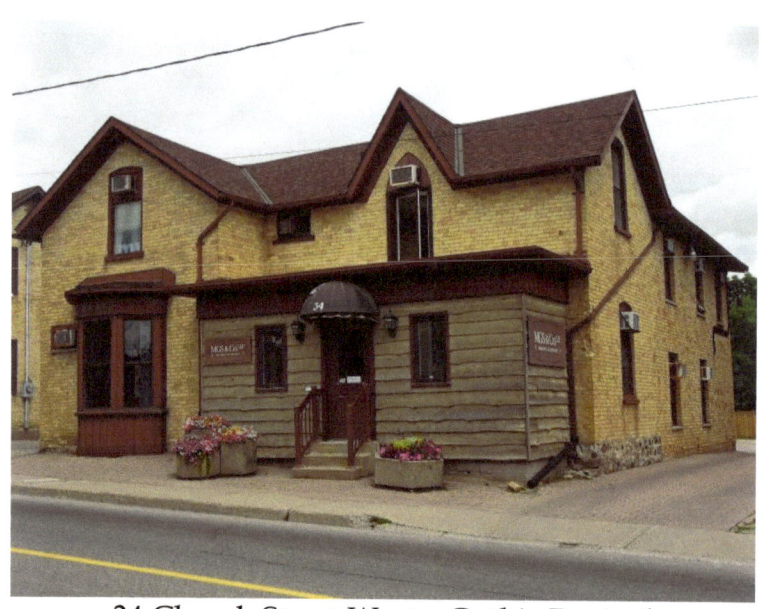

34 Church Street West – Gothic Revival

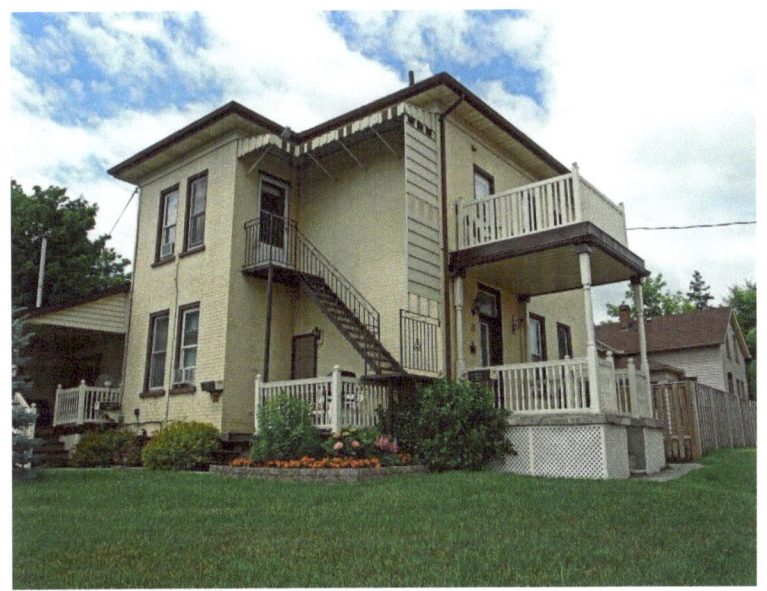

37 Church Street West - Italianate

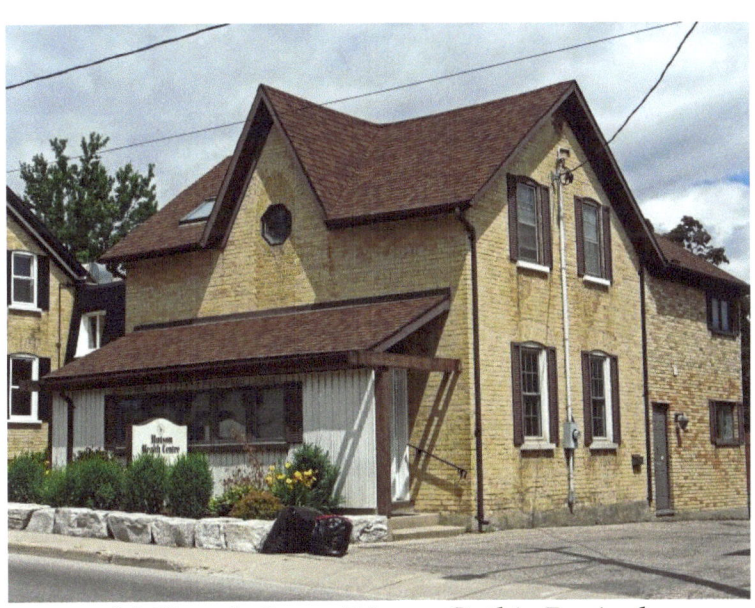

36 Church Street West – Gothic Revival

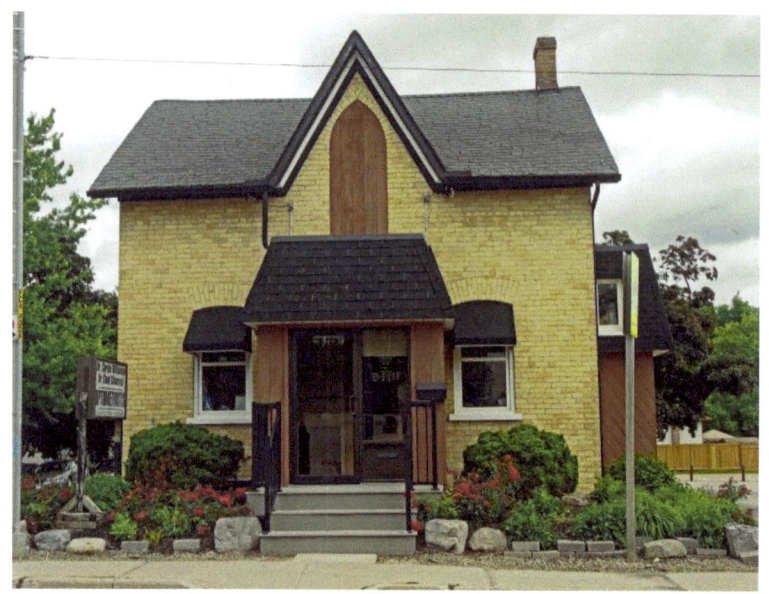

38 Church Street West – Gothic Revival

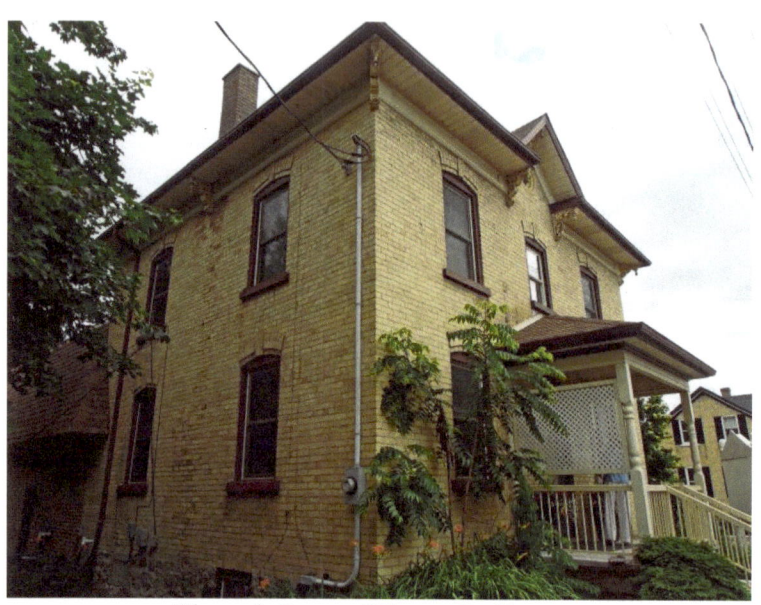

Church Street West - Italianate

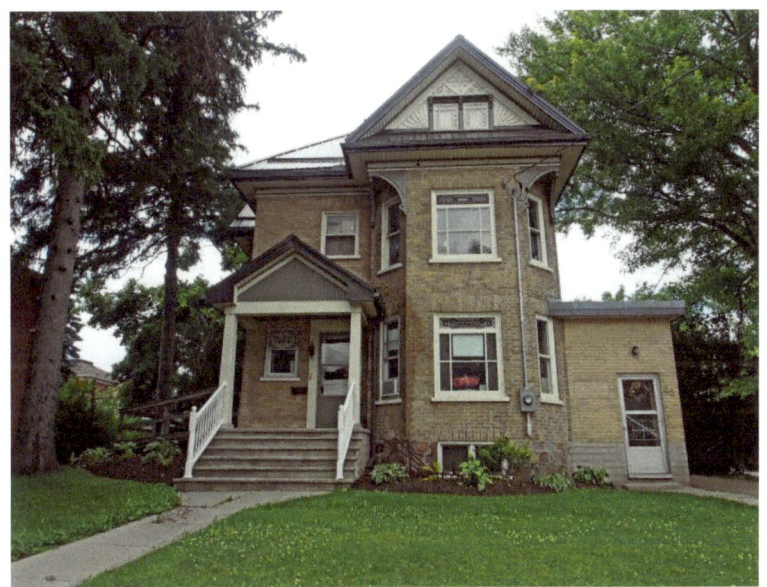

Church Street West

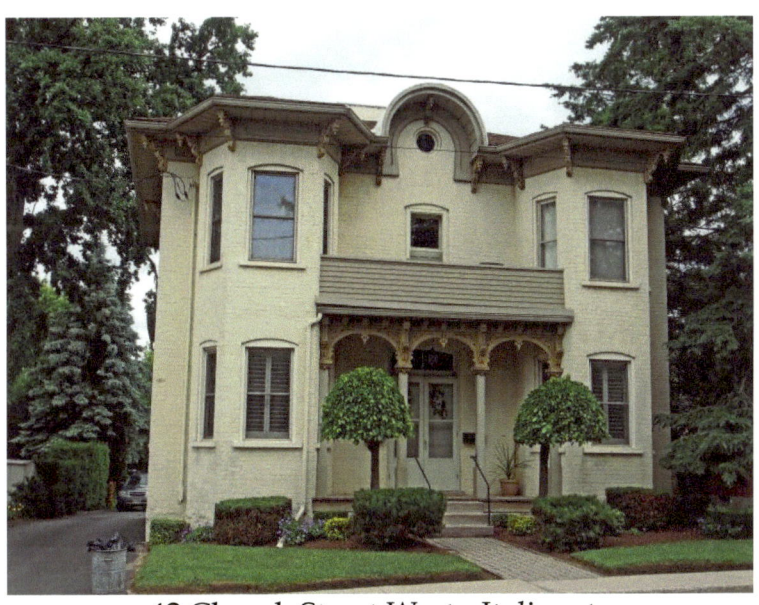

42 Church Street West - Italianate

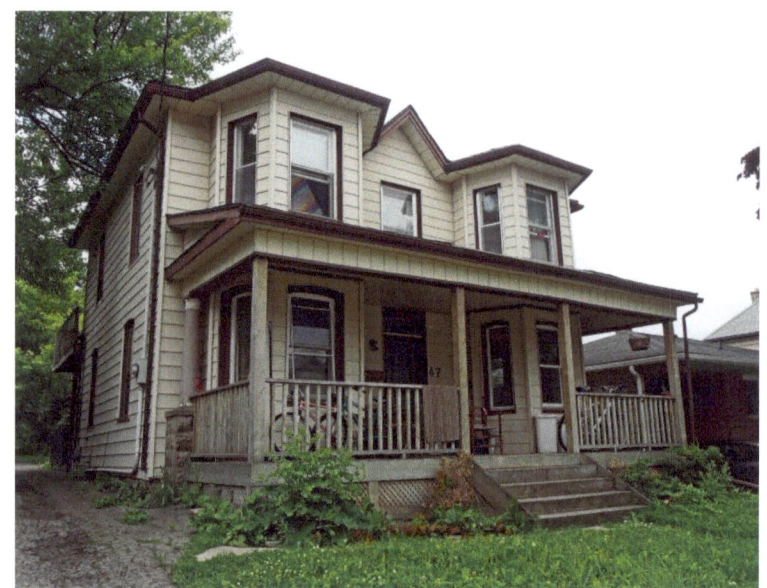

47 Church Street West – Italianate with a two-storey tower-like bay on either side of the entrance

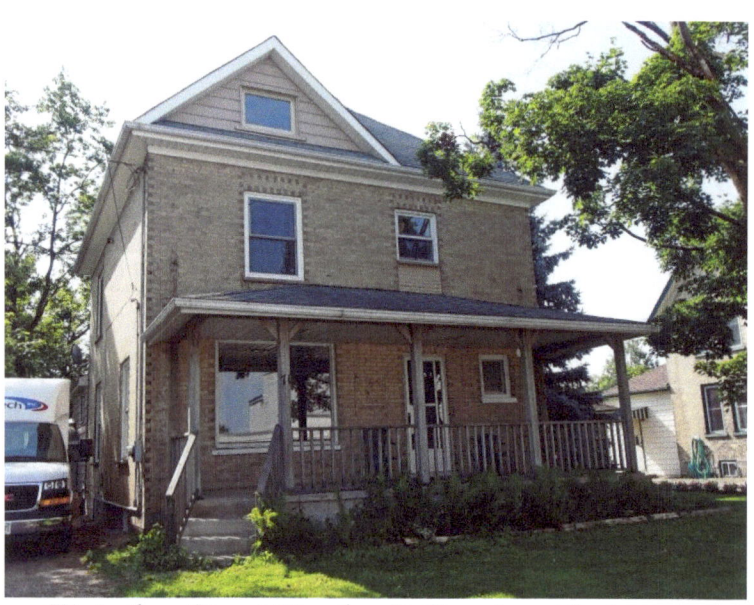

71 Arthur Street North – Italianate with dormer

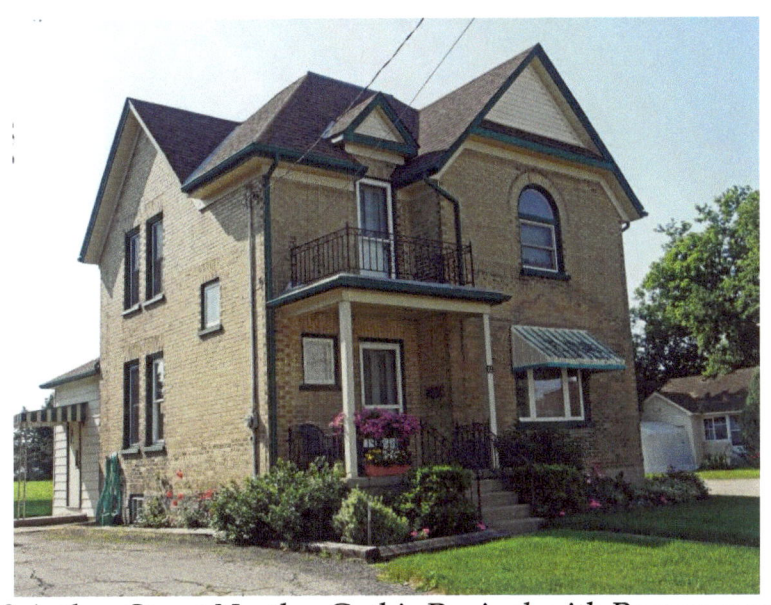

69 Arthur Street North – Gothic Revival with Romanesque style window arch on upper front window

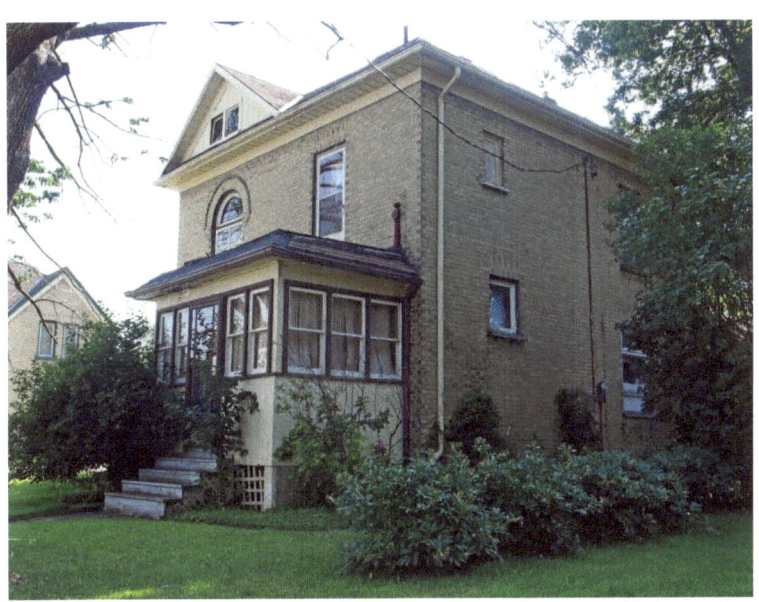

Arthur Street North – Italianate with Romanesque style window arch on upper front window, dormer

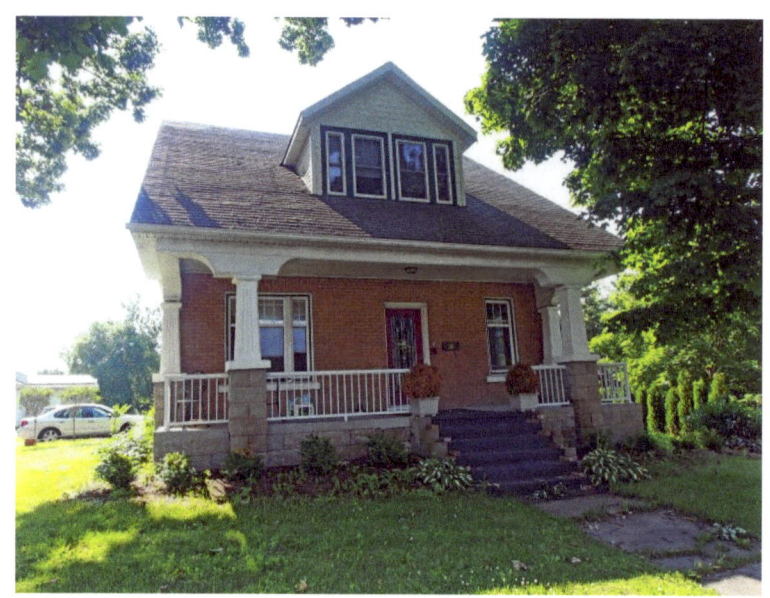

61 Arthur Street North – dormer in attic

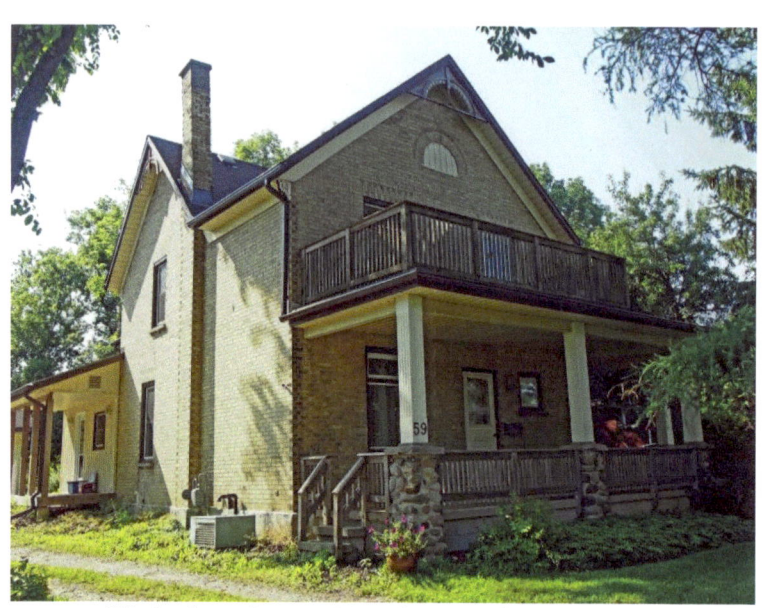

59 Arthur Street North – Gothic Revival,
balcony on second floor

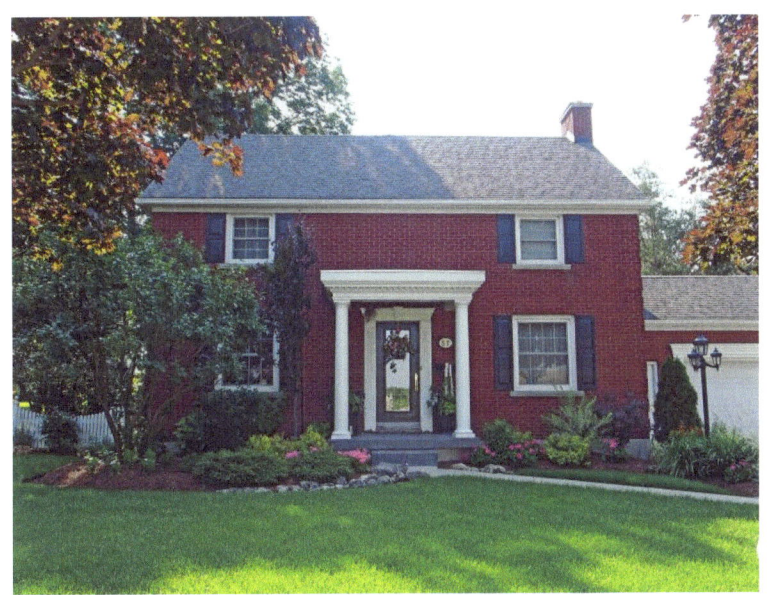

57 Arthur Street North - Georgian

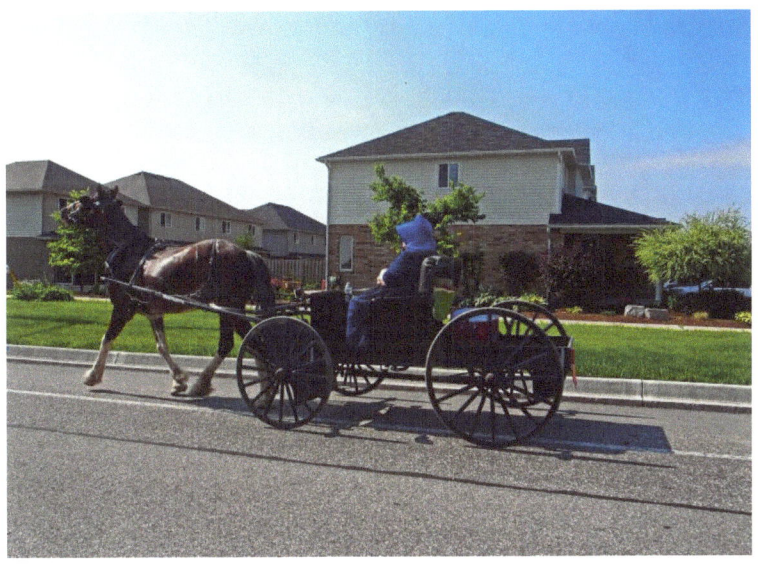

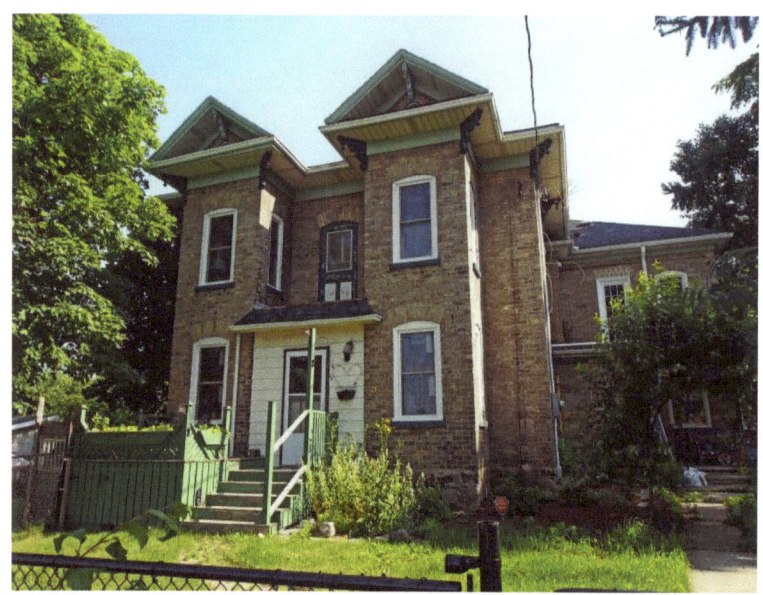

Martins Line – Italianate with two-and-a-half storey tower-like bays, cornice brackets

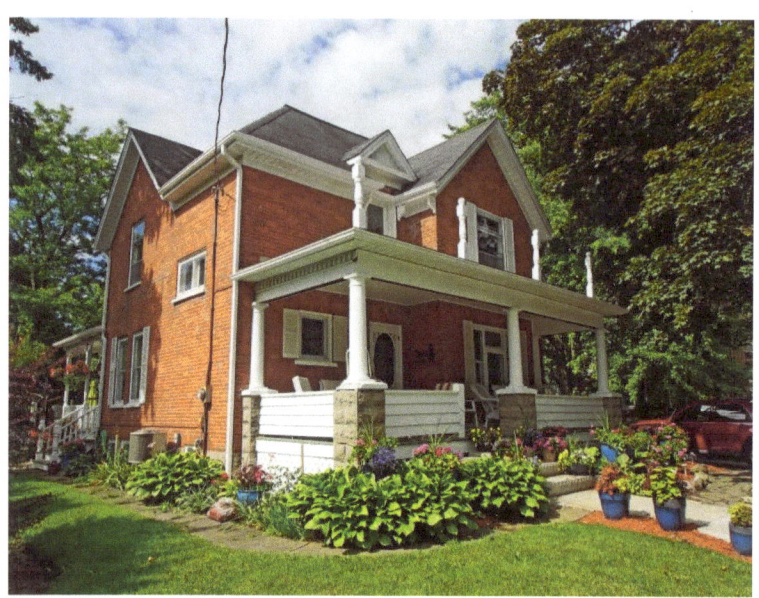

Ernst Street – Gothic Revival

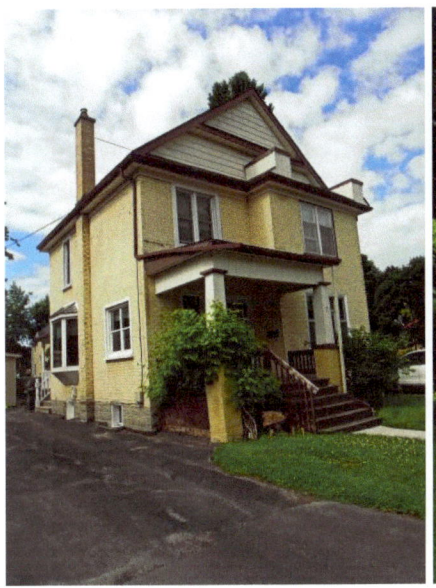
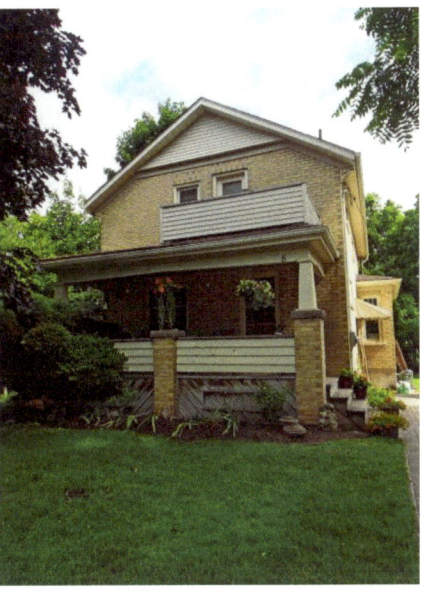

7 Ernst Street
Edwardian

8 Ernst Street
Gothic

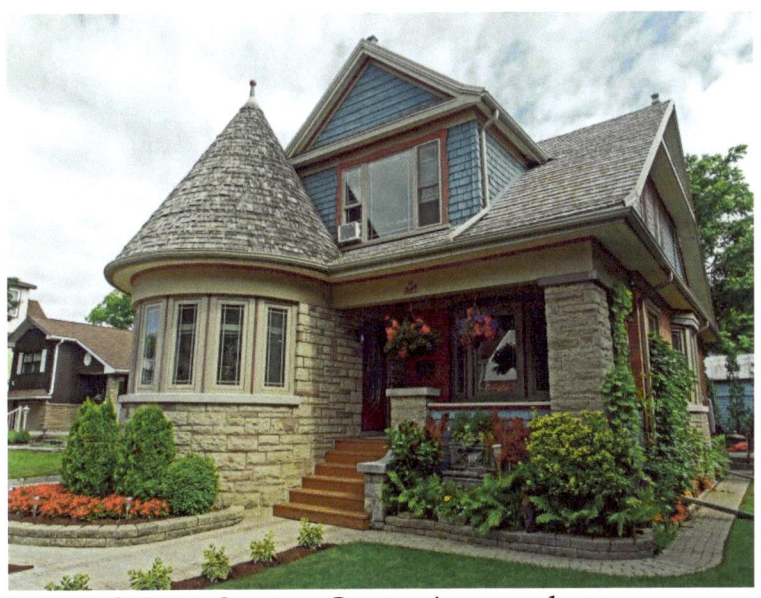

12 Ernst Street – Queen Anne style, turret

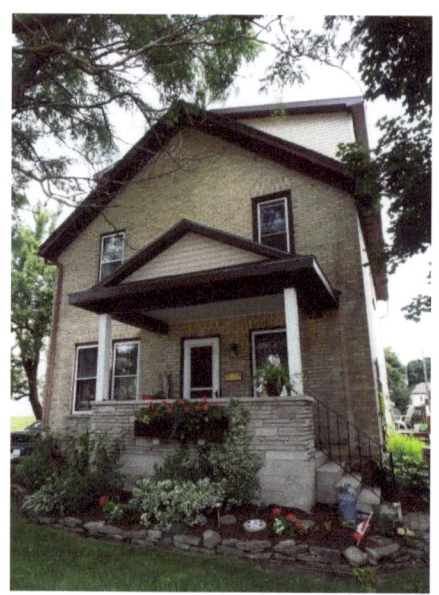

16 Ernst Street – Gothic Revival

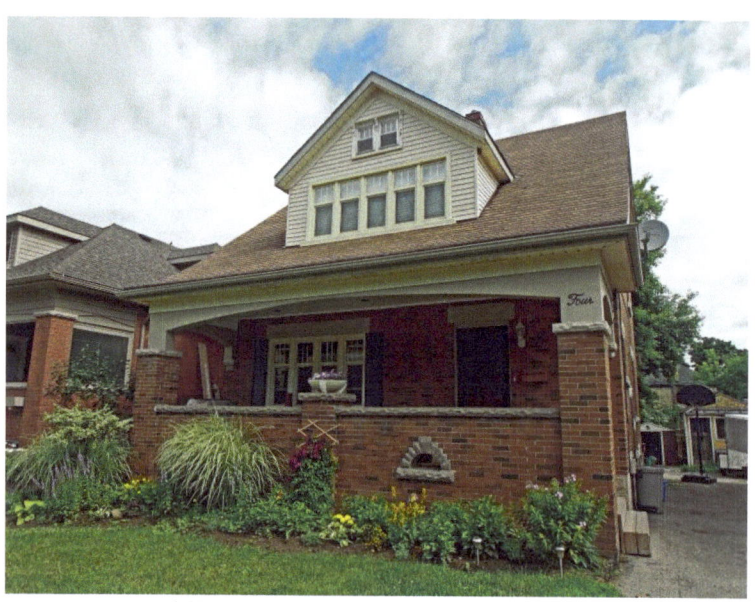

4 Ernst Street – dormer in attic

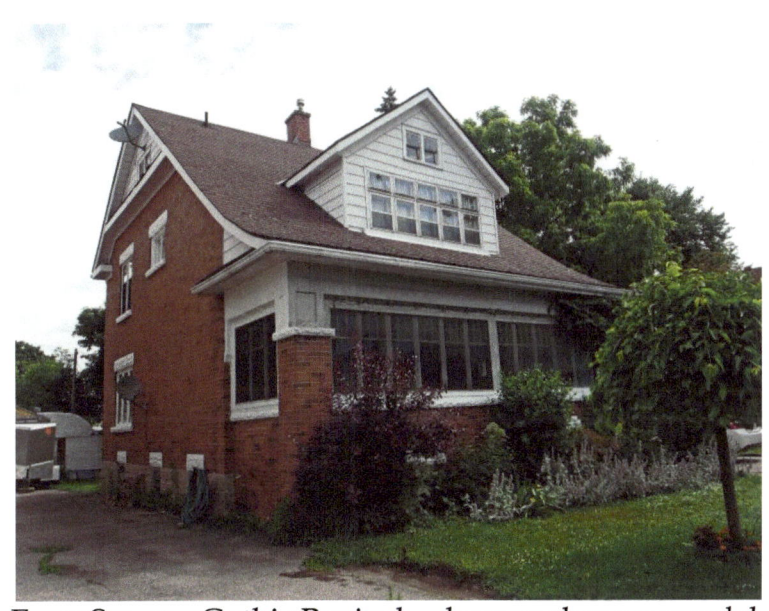

Ernst Street – Gothic Revival – dormer above verandah

Hawkesville

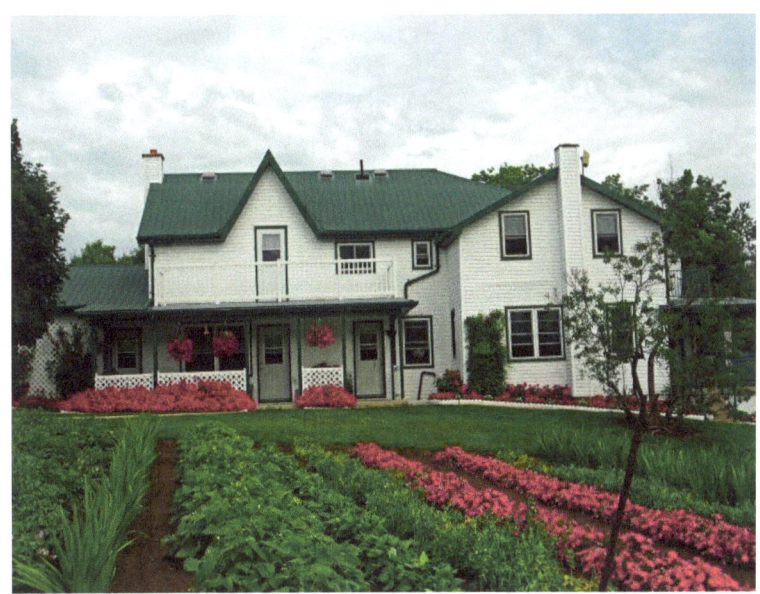

On the highway – Mennonite farm

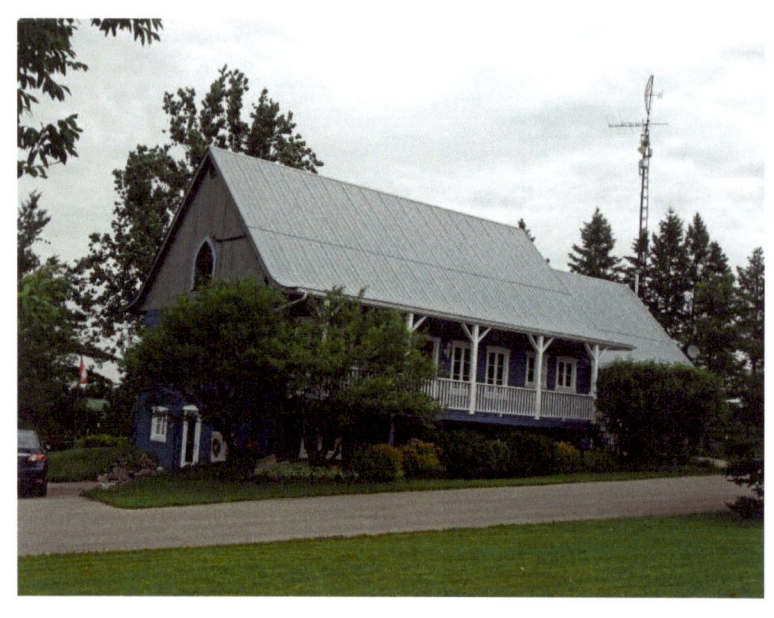

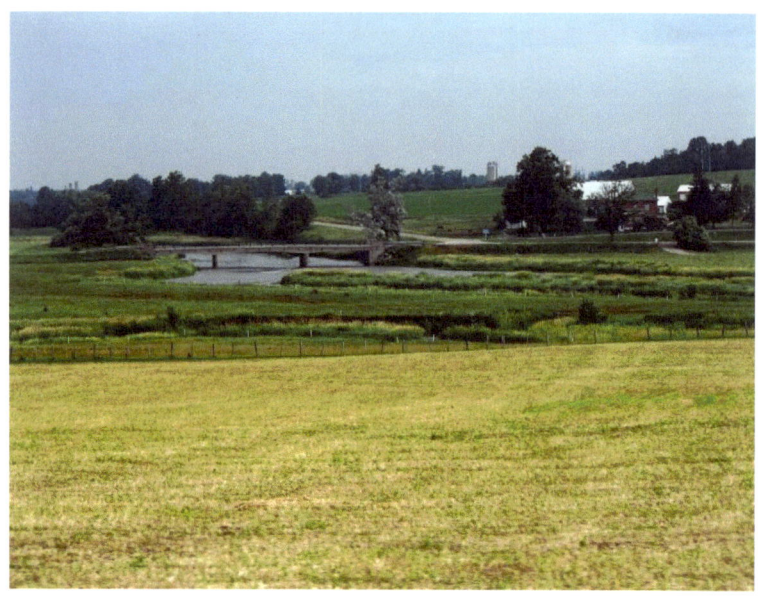

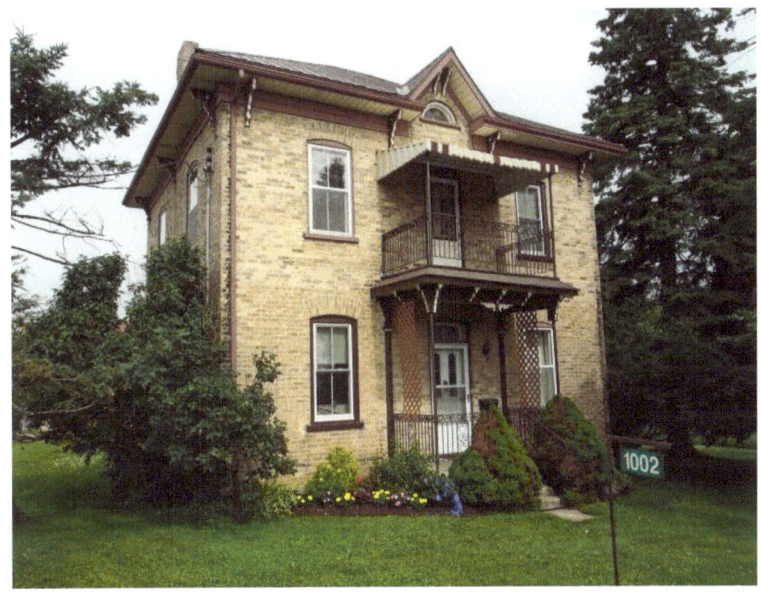

#1002 – Italianate, cornice brackets, balcony on second floor

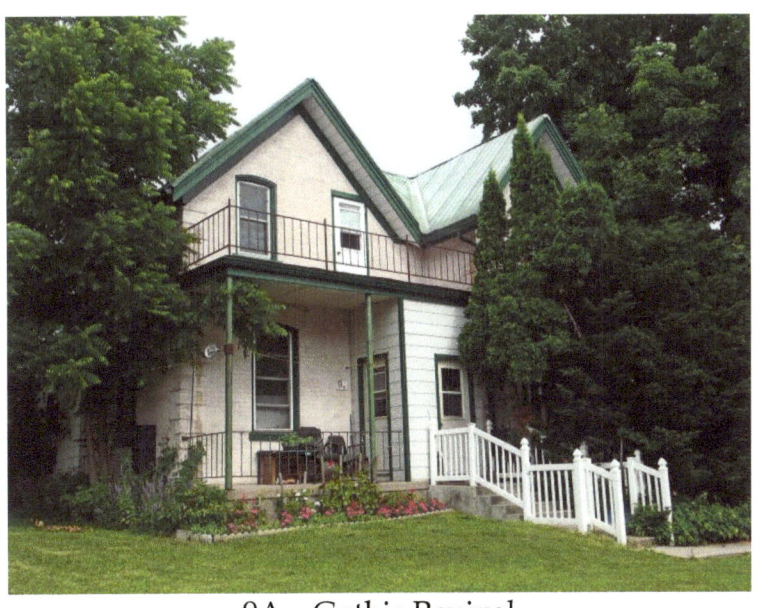

9A – Gothic Revival

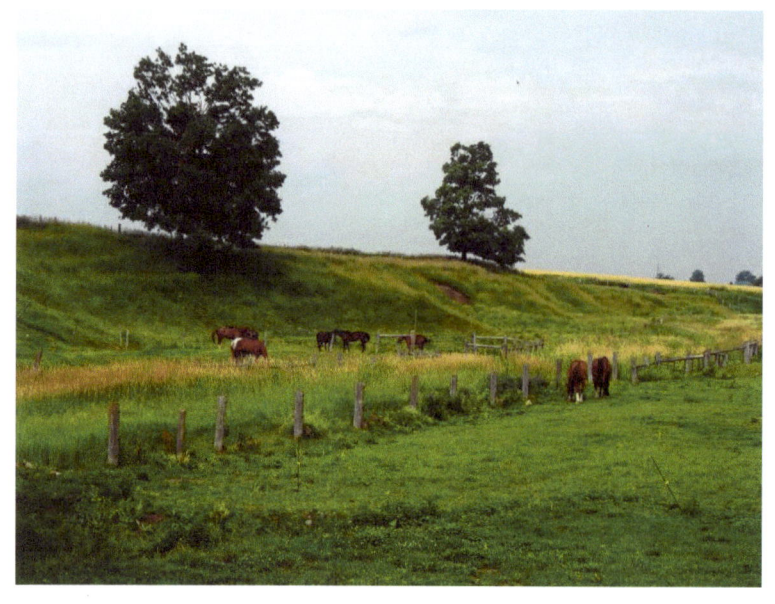

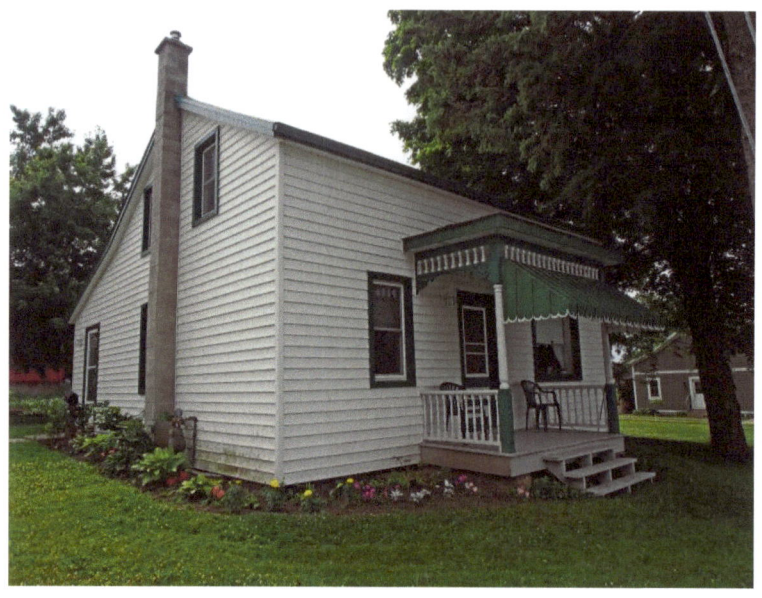

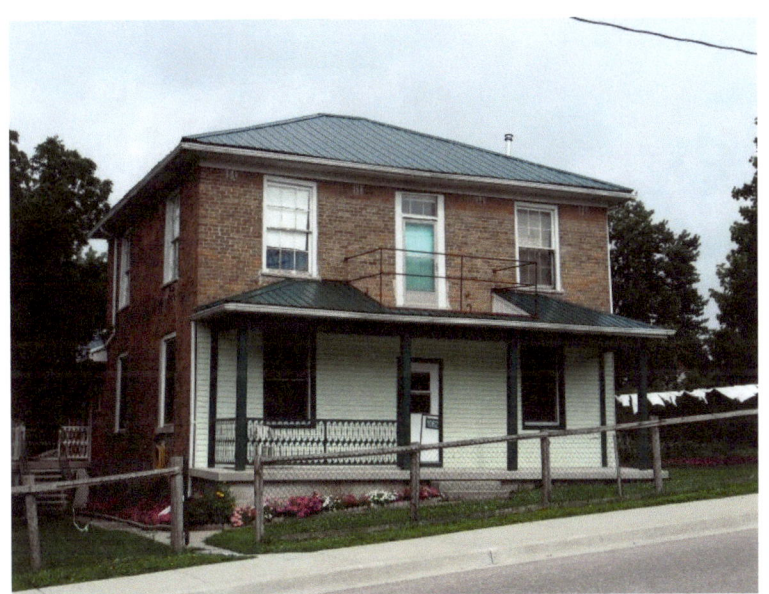

1062 – Italianate – hip roof

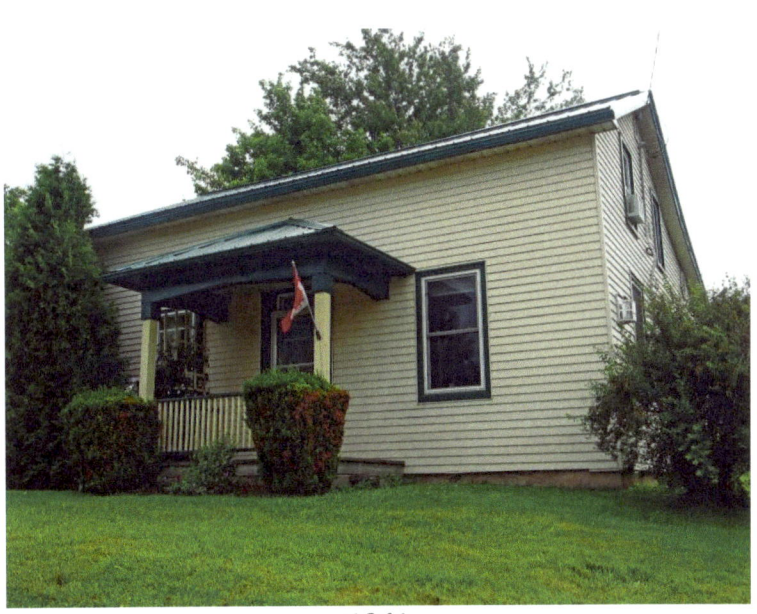

1061

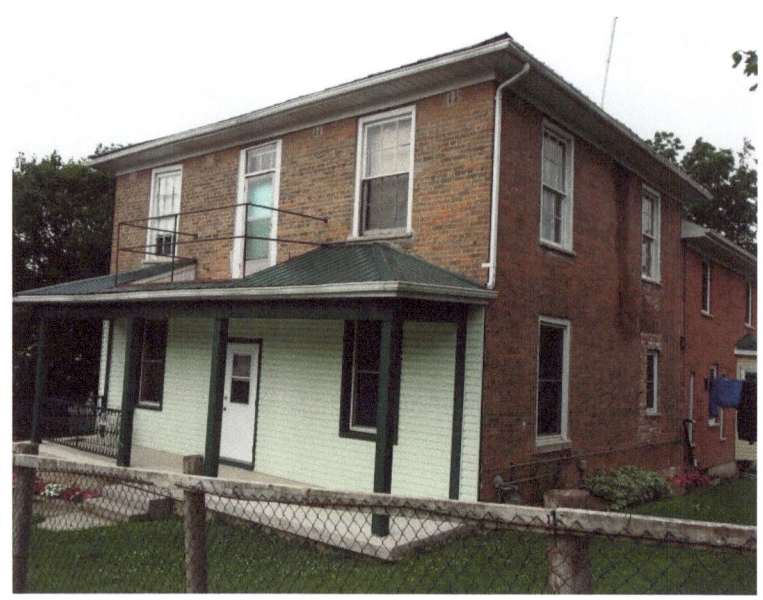

Italianate

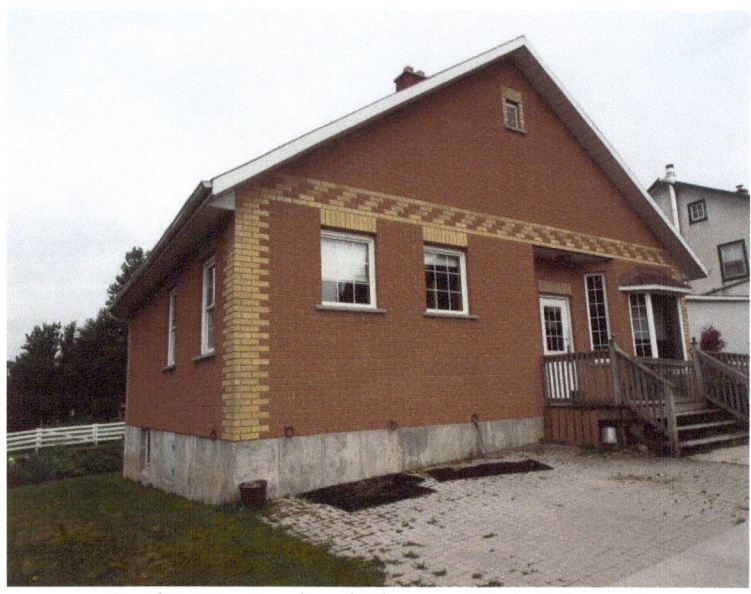

Gothic Revival – dichromatic brickwork

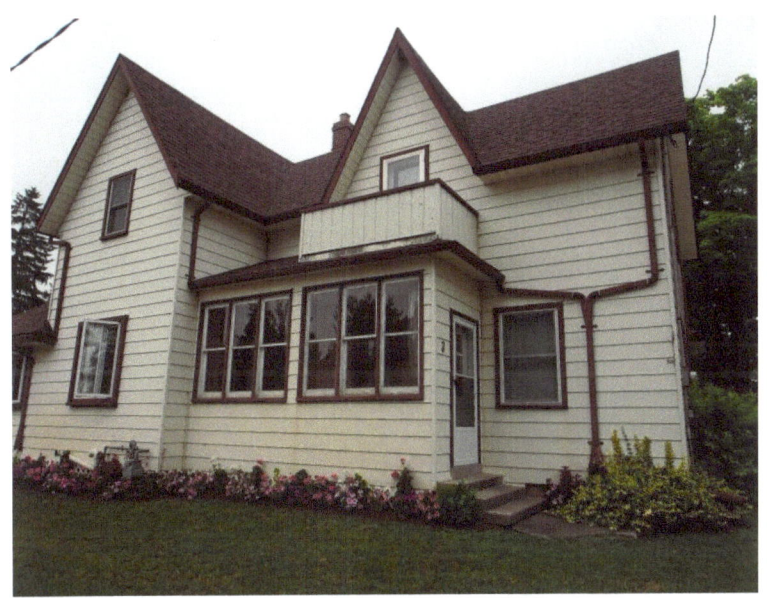

#3 – Gothic Revival

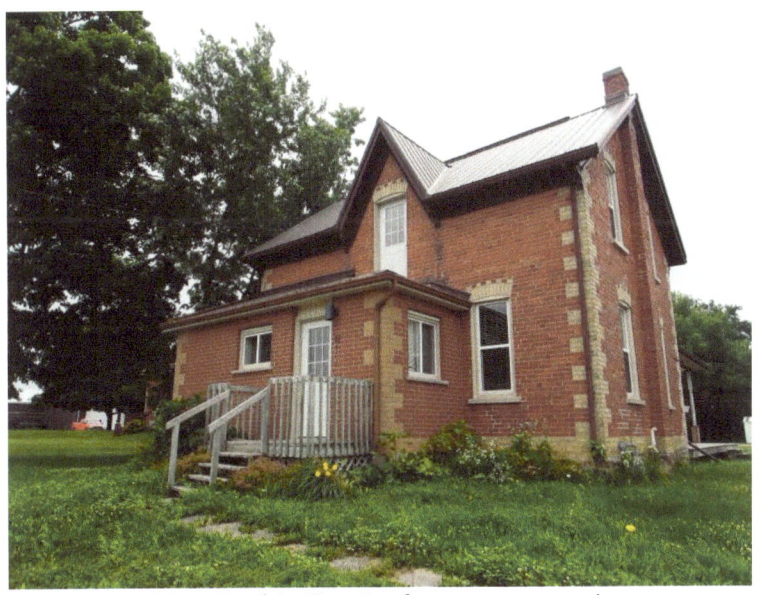

#11 – Gothic Revival – corner quoins

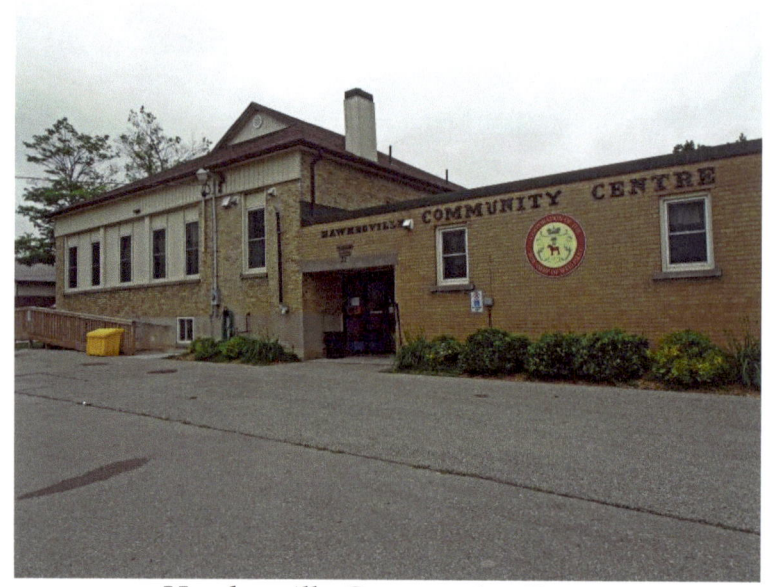

Hawkesville Community Centre

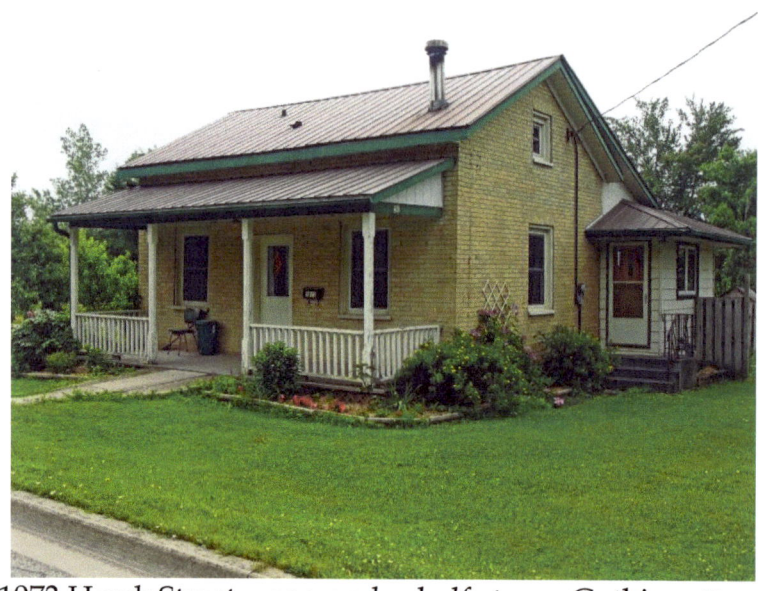

1073 Hawk Street – one-and-a-half storey Gothic cottage

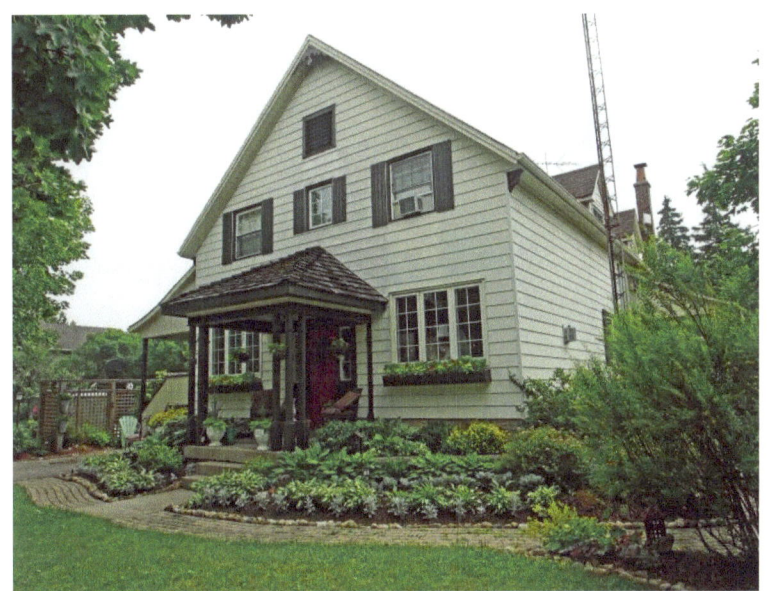

Gothic Revival

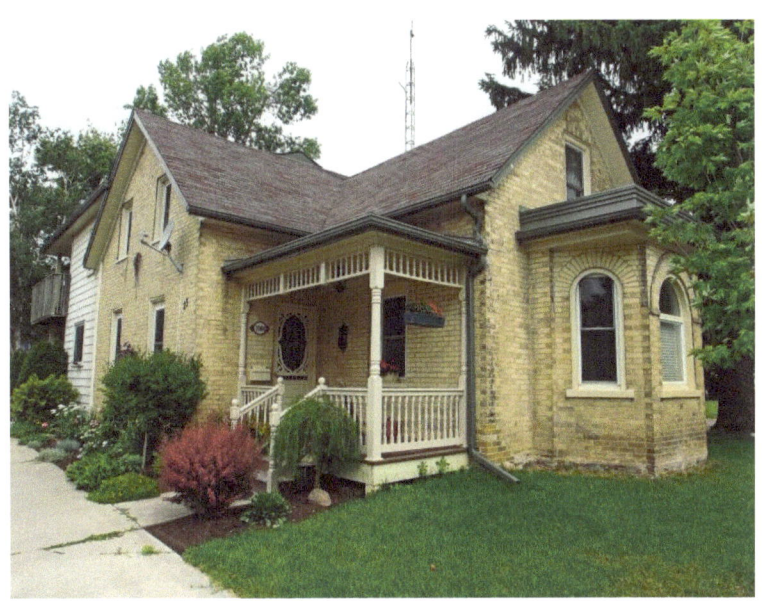

1084 Hawk Street – Gothic Revival, yellow brick

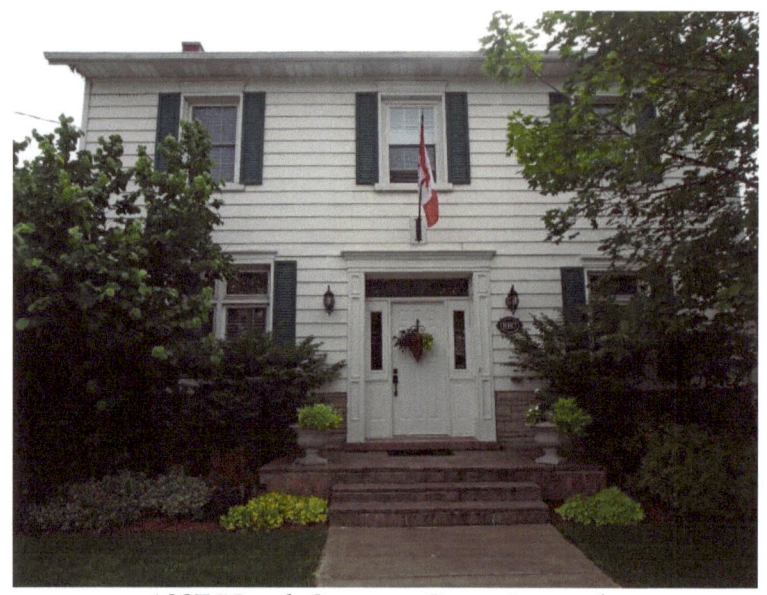

1087 Hawk Street – Georgian style

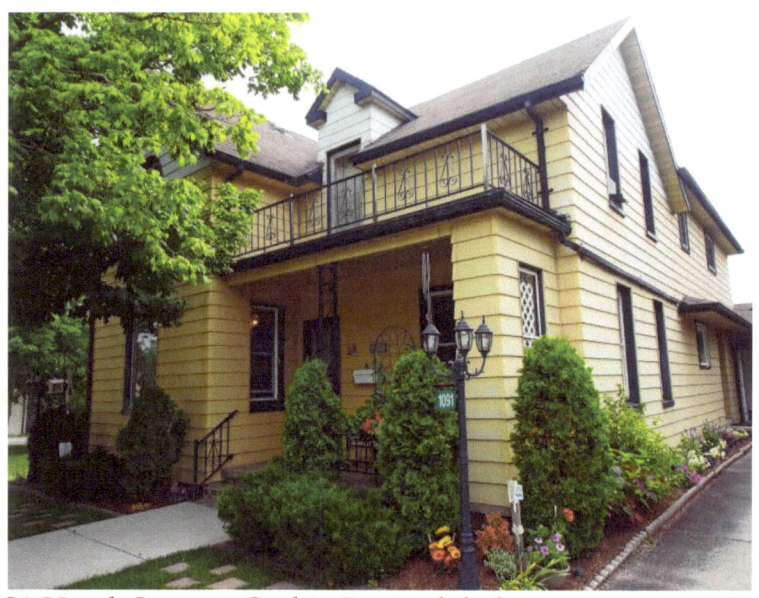

1091 Hawk Street – Gothic Revival, balcony on second floor
with walkout from dormer

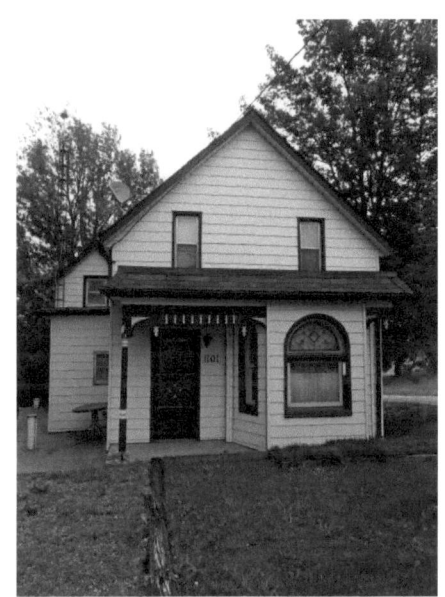

1101 Hawk Street – Gothic Revival

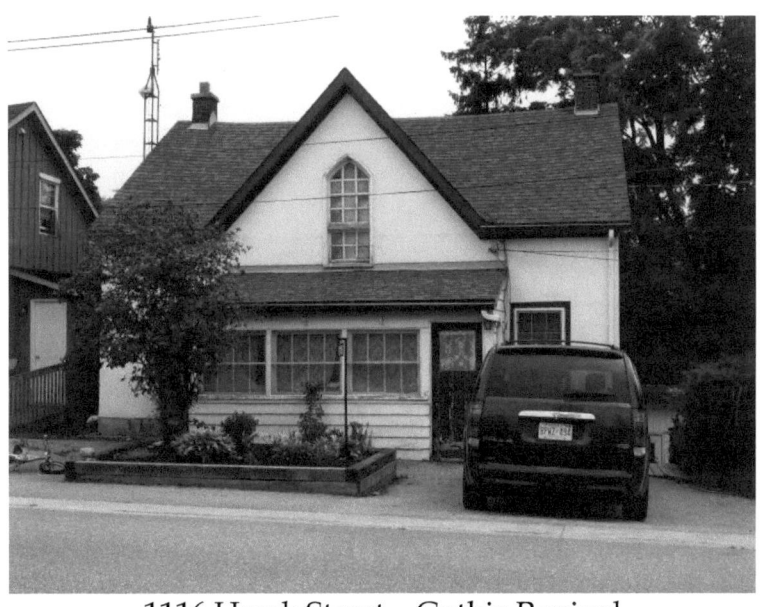

1116 Hawk Street – Gothic Revival

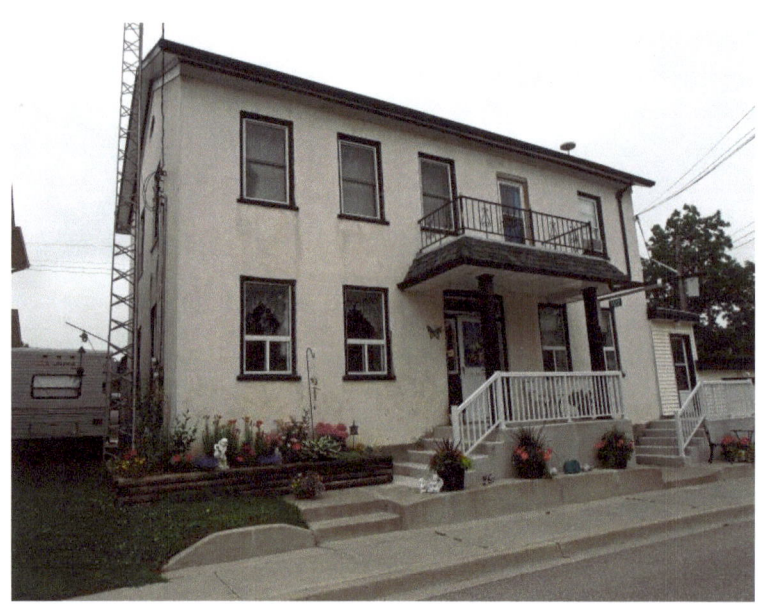

1122 Hawk Street - Georgian

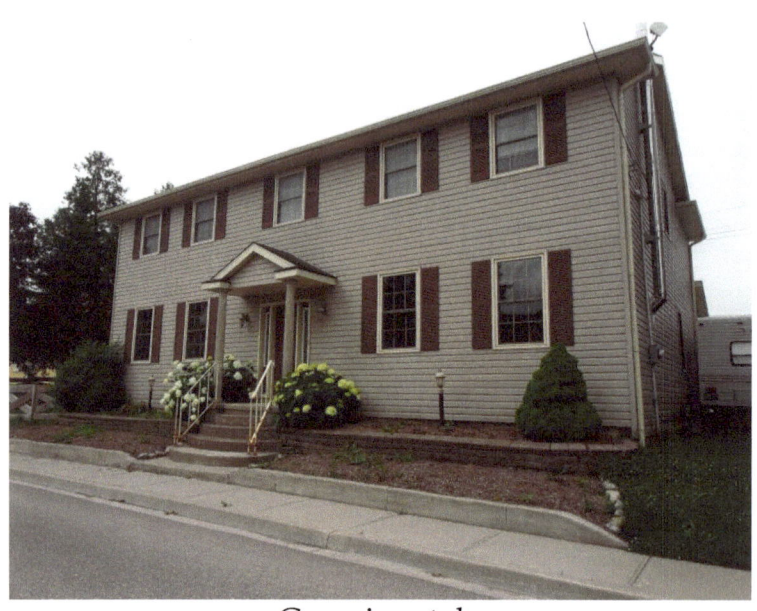

Georgian style

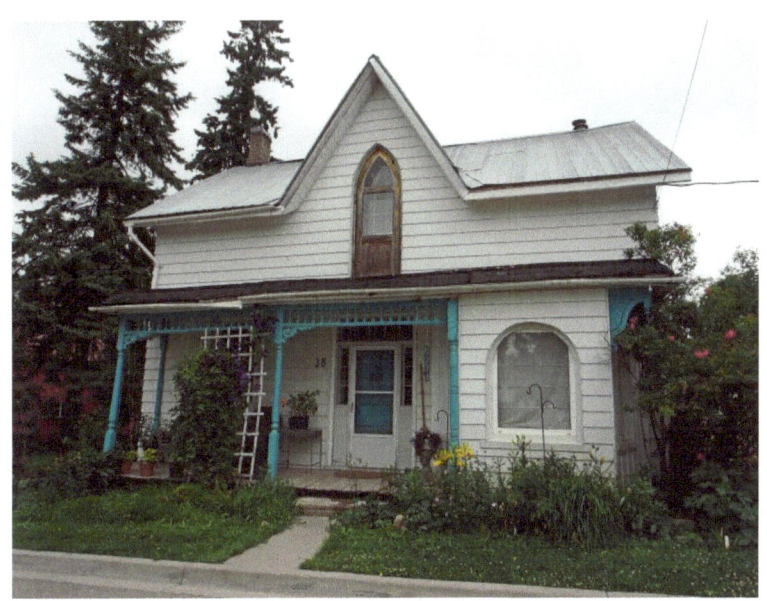

38 Hawk Street – Gothic Revival

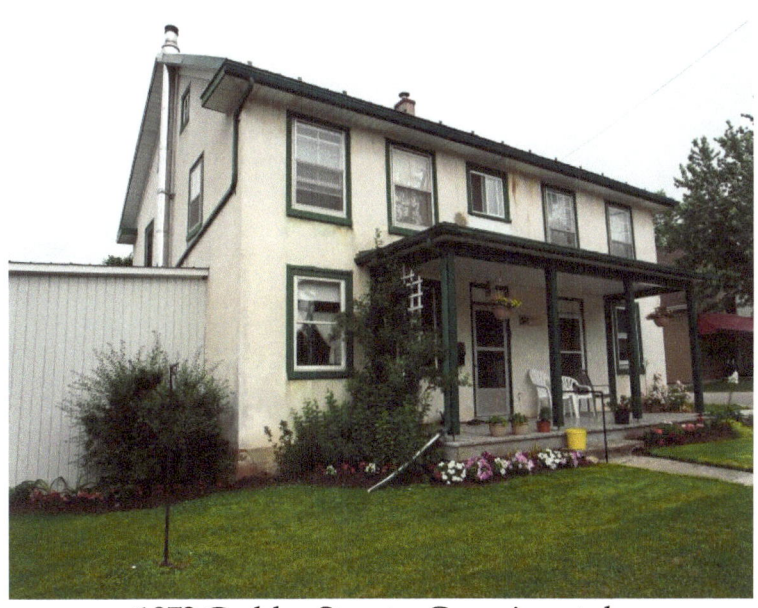

1072 Geddes Street – Georgian style

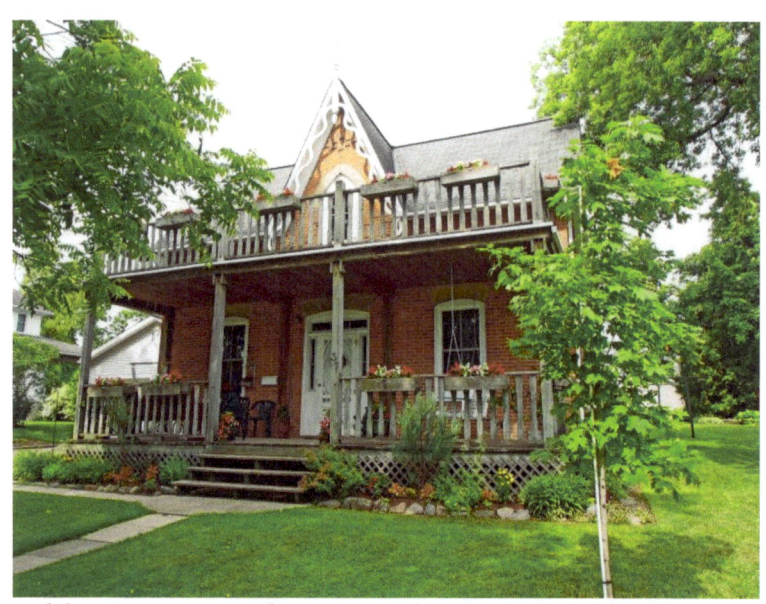

37 Geddes Street – Gothic Revival – Vergeboard trim on gable, second floor balcony

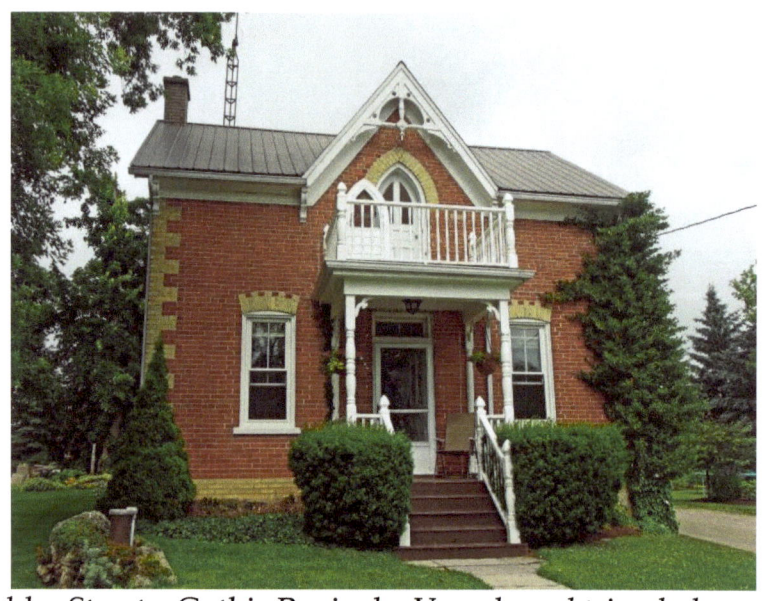

Geddes Street – Gothic Revival – Vergeboard trim, balcony on second floor, corner quoins

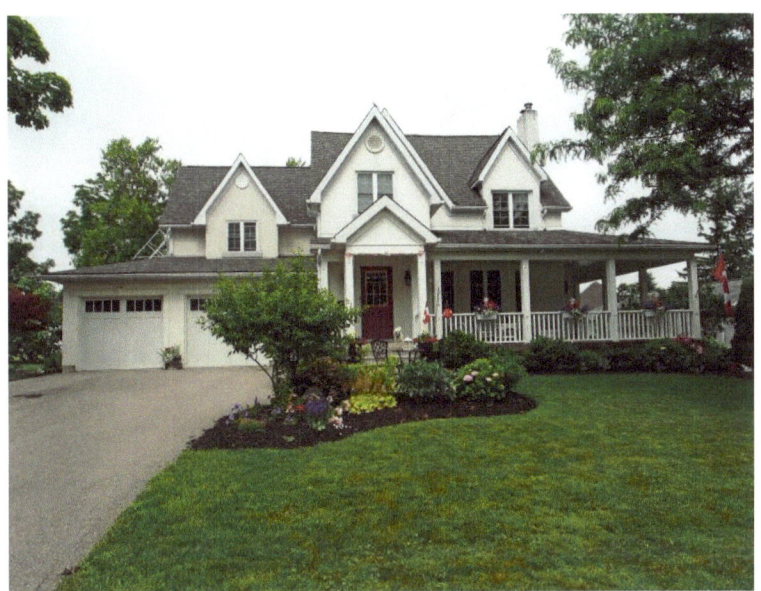

Diefenbacher Street – Gothic Revival

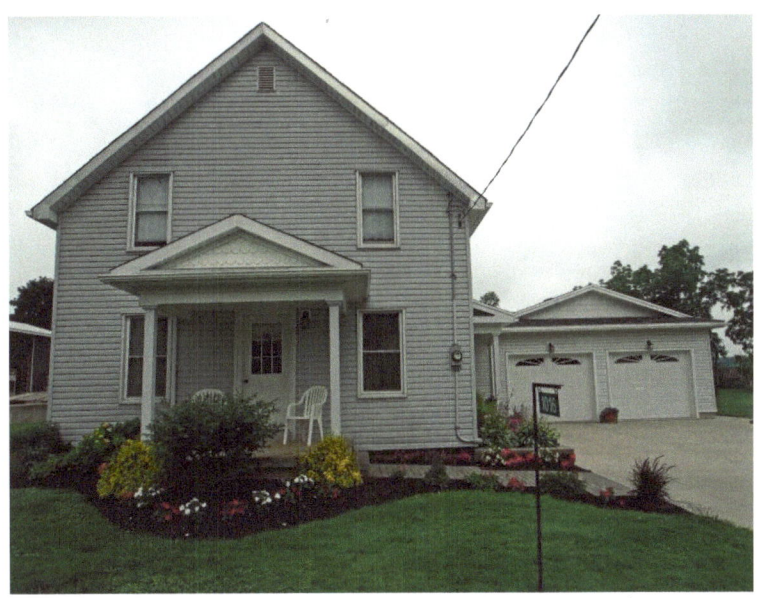

Diefenbacher Street – Gothic Revival

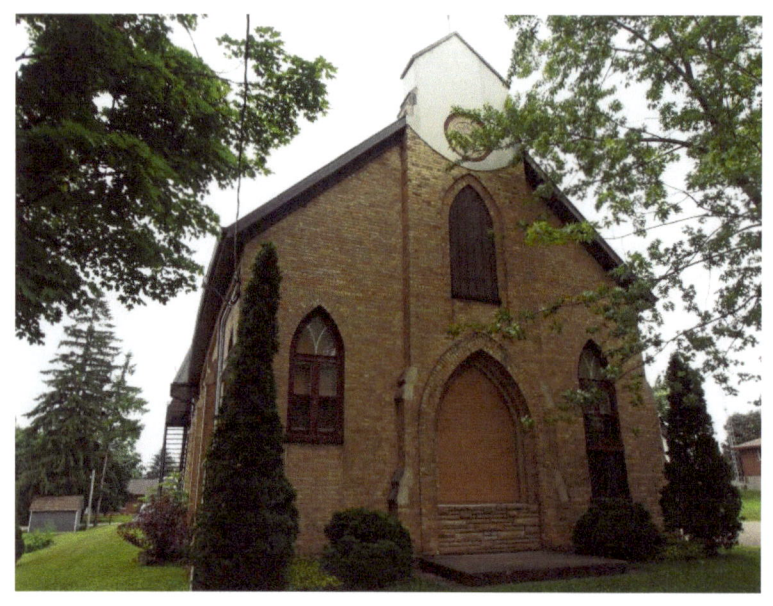

Presbyterian Church c. 1888 - Diefenbacher Street

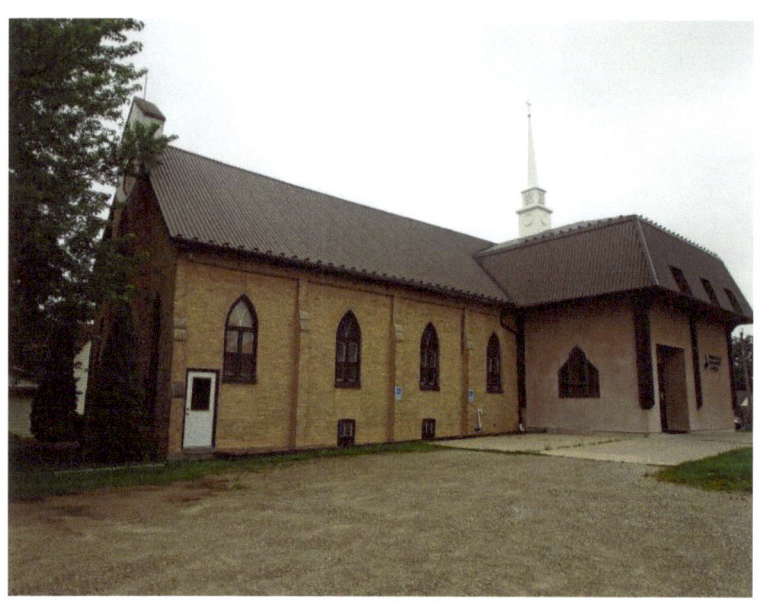

Lancet windows

Wallenstein

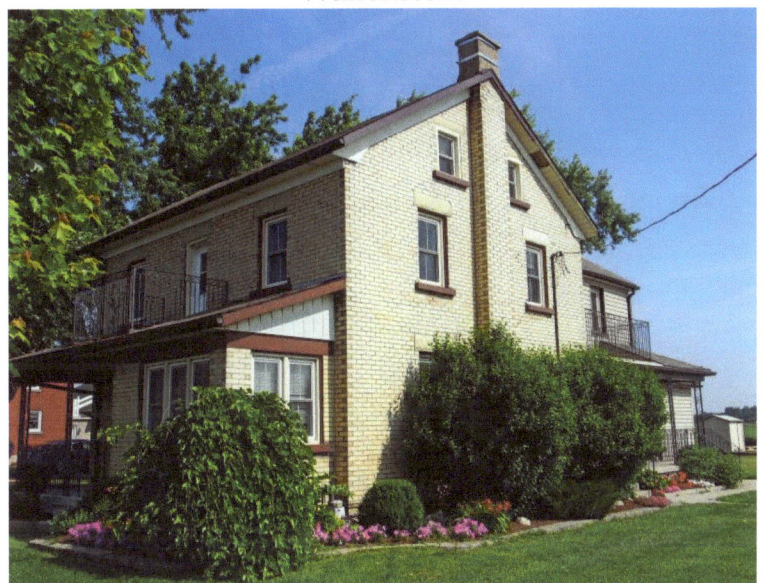

#7217

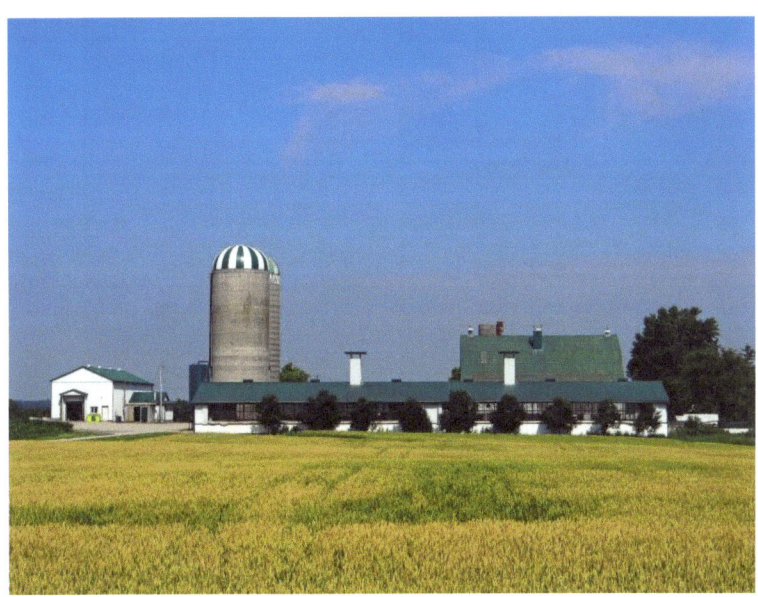

Mennonite Farm

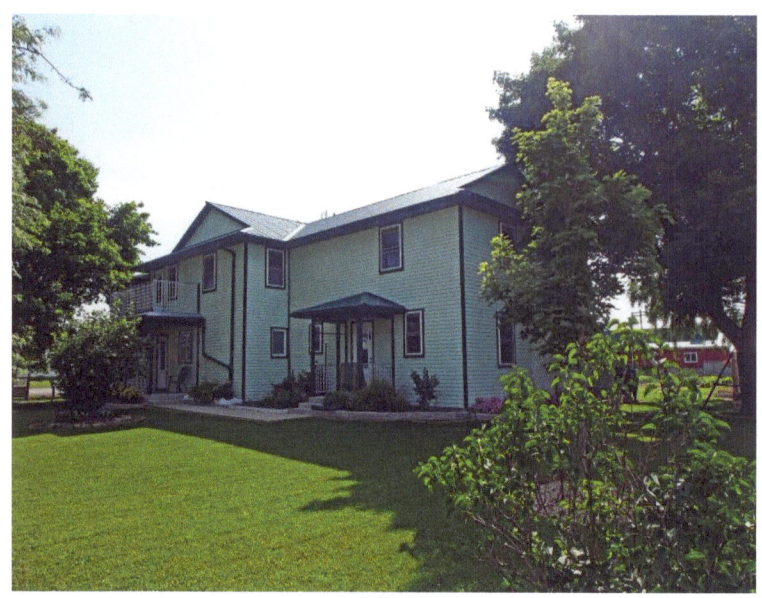

#4711

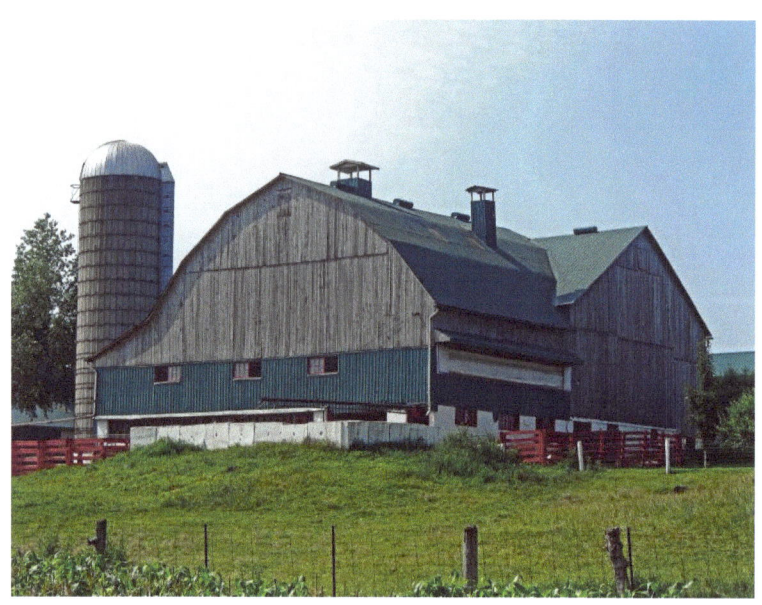

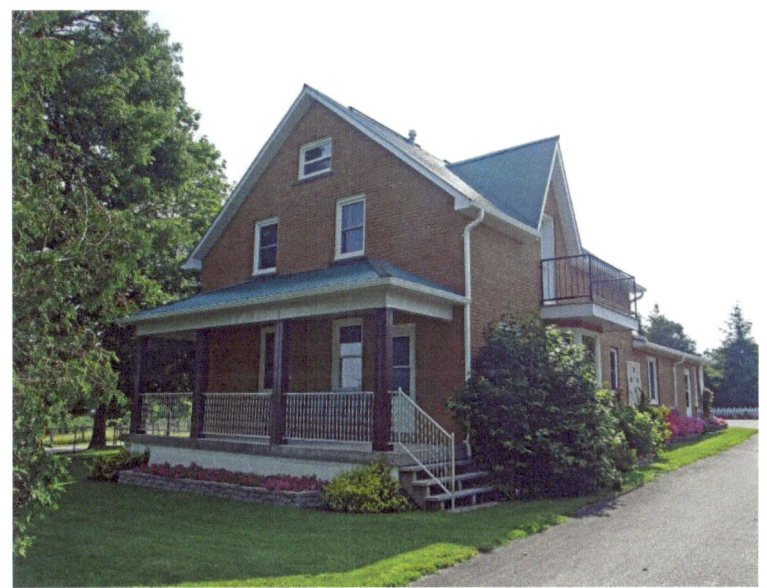

#6381 – Gothic Revival – balcony on second floor

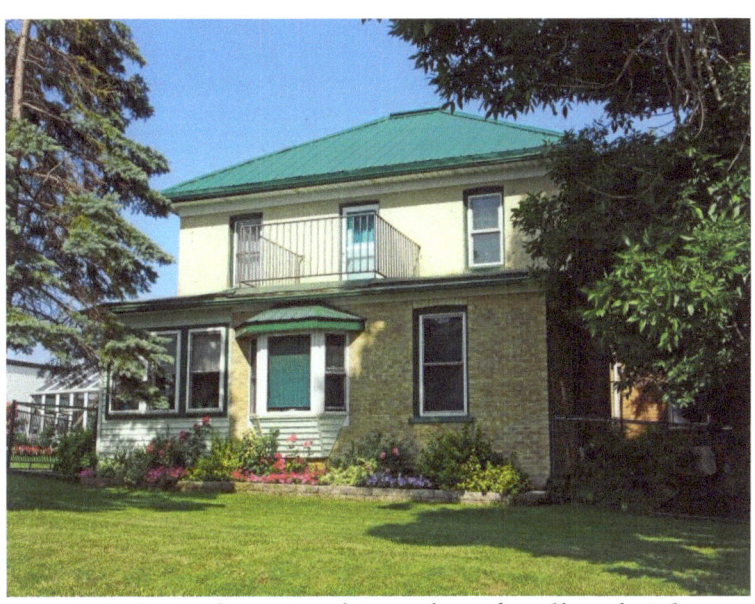

#6378 – Italianate – hipped roof, yellow brick

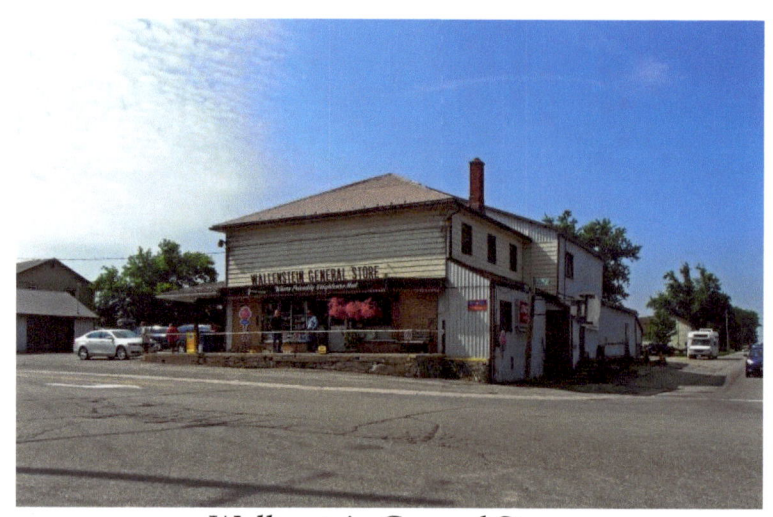

Wallenstein General Store

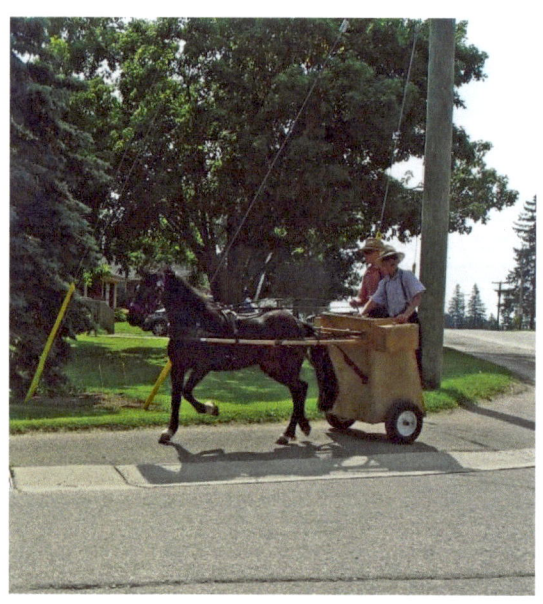

Architectural Terms

Brackets: a decorative or weight-bearing structural element which forms a right angle with one side against a wall and the other under a projecting surface such as an eave or roof. Example: 12 Hampton Street, Elmira	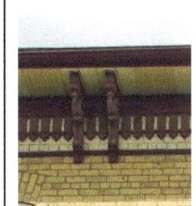
Cornice: originally the wooden overhang of the roof. With the use of stone, brick, iron and steel, the cornice is any projecting shelf at the top of a ceiling or roof. They can be very decorative. Example: 25 Park Avenue, Elmira	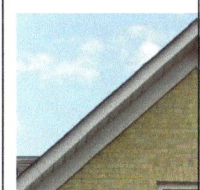
Cornice Return: decorative element on the end of a gable. Example: 38 Hampton Street, Elmira	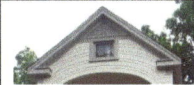
Dichromatic brickwork: the use of two colours of brick, tile or slate to decorate a façade. Example: Hawkesville	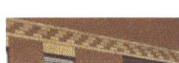
Dormer: (French for "sleep") a gable end window that pierces through the plane of a sloping roof surface to create usable space in the top floor or attic of a building by adding headroom. Example: 61 Arthur Street North, Elmira	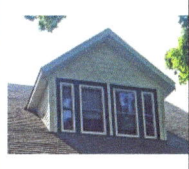

Gable: the triangular portion of a wall between the edges of a sloping roof. Example: 5 Park Avenue, Elmira	
Hipped Roof: a roof where all sides slope downwards to the walls with no gables. Example: #6378, Wallenstein	
Lancet Window: a tall, narrow window with a pointed arch at its top. Example: Presbyterian Church, Diefenbacher Street, Hawkesville	
Palladian Window: a large window that is divided into three sections with the centre section larger than the two side sections and usually arched. Example: 6 Hampton Street, Elmira	
Pediment: a triangular section above the horizontal structure (entablature), typically supported by columns. The inside of the triangle is called the tympanum.	

Quoin: masonry blocks at the corner of a wall, often a decorative feature, usually larger or of a different colour than the rest of the wall. Example: Hawkesville	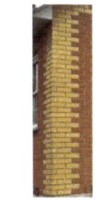
Turret: a small tower that projects from the wall of a building. Example: 12 Ernst Street, Elmira	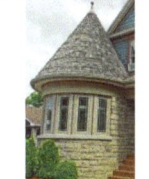
Vergeboard and Finial: also called bargeboards – hang from the projecting end of a roof and are often elaborately carved and ornamented. **Finial:** ornament added to the top of a gable, pinnacle, canopy or spire – a Gothic element. Example: 37 Geddes Street, Hawkesville	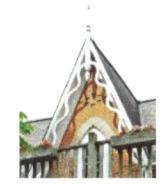

Elmira Building Styles

Edwardian, 1900-1930 – This style bridges the ornate and elaborate styles of the Victorian era and the simplified styles of the 20th century. Balanced facades, simple roof lines, dormer windows, large front porches, and smooth brick surfaces are its characteristics. Example: 10 Hampton Street, Elmira	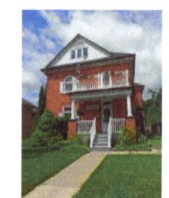
Georgian, before 1860 – This style began with the British King Georges in the 18th century. These buildings have balanced facades around a central door, medium-pitched gable roofs, and small paned windows. Example: 1087 Hawk Street, Hawkesville	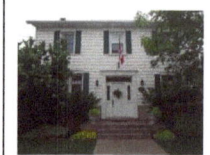
Gothic Revival, 1830-1890 – These decorative buildings have sharply-pitched gables with highly detailed vergeboards, pointed-arch window openings, and dichromatic brickwork. It is a common style in Ontario. Example: 32 Hampton Street, Elmira	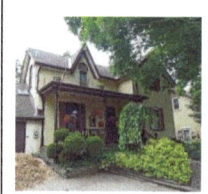
Italianate, 1850-1900 – It has wide-bracketed eaves, belvederes, wrap-around verandahs. Example: 37 Church Street West, Elmira	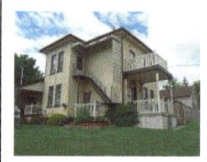

Queen Anne, 1885-1900 – This style is distinguished by an irregular outline featuring a combination of an offset tower, broad gables, projecting two-storey bays, verandahs, multi-sloped roofs, and tall, decorative chimneys. A mixture of brick and wood is common. Windows often have one large single-paned bottom sash and small panes in the upper sash. Example: 12 Ernst Street, Elmira	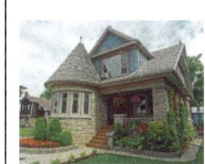
Romanesque Revival, 1880-1910 – This style hearkens back to medieval architecture of the 11th and 12th centuries with a heavy appearance, blocky towers and rounded arches. Romanesque style arch Example: 7 Park Avenue, Elmira	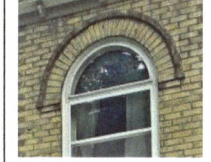

www.ingramcontent.com/pod-product-compliance
Lightning Source LLC
Chambersburg PA
CBHW040855180526
45159CB00001B/428